I0307648

(7) SEVEN NOTE GUITAR

BY CHAD R. VILLEGAS

COPYRIGHT © CHAD R. VILLEGAS 2019

ALL RIGHTS RESERVED

(7) SEVEN NOTE GUITAR

COPYRIGHT © CHAD R. VILLEGAS 2019

ALL RIGHTS RESERVED

THE UNAUTHORIZED REPRODUCTION, DISTRIBUTION OR INFRINGEMENT OF THIS COPYRIGHTED MATERIAL IS PROHIBITED

ISBN: 978-1-7330360-1-6

TABLE OF CONTENTS

INTRODUCTION	1
CHORDS	3
INTERVALS	7
SCALES / MODES	12
EXTENDED CHORDS	15
MORE MODES	21
POWER CHORDS	25
AUGMENTED/DIMINISHED/SUSPENDED CHORDS	29
DYAD CHORDS	36
BLUES	44
MORE DYAD CHORDS	48
CHORD KEYS	55

(7) SEVEN NOTE GUITAR

Music is the replication of sounds that occur in nature. Every sound that is heard in nature has a sound quality that has been observed with great intent. These sound qualities are consistant in that they always have and always will be the same, forever. This consistency has allowed sound qualities to be replicated using musical instruments. Musical instruments allow natural sounds to be played. Musical instruments play either single sounds called notes or multiple sounds played together called chords.

In music, notes are single sounds that play alone or are played with other notes. The combining of notes played together are called chords. Chords combined with other chords are called chord progressions. Chord progressions vary in size; from two chord progressions to multi-chord progressions; also from single instruments playing chords to multi-instruments each playing single notes while all playing together forming chords.

Simply understanding seven (7) notes is an idea that leads to the thought of an eighth (8) note, also known as an octave. An octave is a note that starts the same exact seven letter notes at a higher pitch (Hz). Example notes: C, D, E, F, G, A, B and C once more is the eighth note or the first of the same seven letter notes repeated at an octave higer in pitch (Hz). Chosen for example, the key of C major. A key is a set of notes forming a scale from which music is created and composed. The key of C major contains

NO FLAT (b) NOTES, NOR DOES IT CONTAIN SHARP (#) NOTES. THUS, THIS LACK OF FLATS(b) AND SHARPS(#) WILL MAKE EASIER THE UNDERSTANDING OF MUSIC. THE KEY OF C MAJOR CONTAINS THE CHORDS: C MAJOR, D MINOR, E MINOR, F MAJOR, G MAJOR, A MINOR AND B DIMINISHED.

THE FOLLOWING INFORMATION WILL HELP IN THE UNDERSTANDING OF THE RELATIONSHIP BETWEEN MUSIC THEORY AND THE PRACTICAL USE OF THE PROVIDED GRIDS AND GRAPHICS. THE FINGERS YOU USE TO FRET CHORDS OR NOTES IS YOUR PREFERENCE. THE IDEA OF FRETTING NOTES AND CHORDS IN DIFFERENT WAYS, USING DIFFERENT FINGERS, IS A GOOD IDEA. IF BIG FINGERS ARE USED TO FRET, THIS FREES UP SMALL FINGERS FOR LIGHTER STRINGS. IF SMALL FINGERS ARE USED TO FRET, THIS FREES UP BIG FINGERS FOR HEAVIER STRINGS. SUGGESTION: PLAY CHORDS AND SCALES AND GIVE YOUR HANDS TIME TO GET USED TO THE PHYSICAL CHALLENGE OF PRACTICING DAILY, TWICE A DAY IF POSSIBLE.

THEORY: TONES AND STEPS ARE TWO DIFFERENT WAYS OF DESCRIBING THE SAME IDEA. WHEN ON ONE GUITAR STRING AND MOVE ONE (1) FRET, YOU ARE MOVING A SEMI-TONE OR A HALF-STEP. WHEN ON ONE GUITAR STRING AND MOVE TWO (2) FRETS, YOU ARE MOVING ONE (1) TONE OR ONE (1) WHOLE STEP. THUS, TWO (2) SEMI-TONES EQUALS ONE (1) TONE OR, TWO (2) HALF-STEPS EQUALS ONE (1) WHOLE STEP. SEMI-TONES AND TONES AS WELL AS HALF-STEPS AND WHOLE STEPS ARE TWO DIFFERENT WAYS OF DESCRIBING THE SAME IDEA.

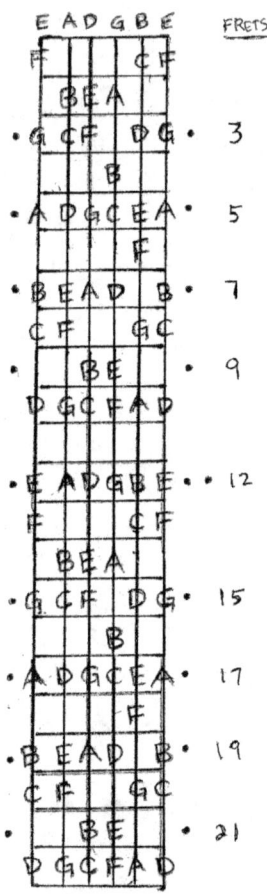

F AND CAGED CHORDS

OPEN CHORDS ARE KNOWN AS CAGED CHORDS, THAT IS C CHORD, A CHORD, G CHORD, E CHORD, AND D CHORD. THE LETTERS C, A, G, E, AND D FORM AN ACRONYM. THE F CHORD IS ALSO A USEFUL SHAPED CHORD AND SHOULD BE INCLUDED. THUS, F AND CAGED CHORDS. THE F CHORD IS A CHORD FRAGMENT OF THE OPEN E CHORD, THIS SHOULD BE RECOGNIZED. HOWEVER, THE USE OF THESE OPEN CHORDS IN A PARTIAL FORM (FRAGMENT) ARE VERY USEFUL FOR CLEAN OR AMPLIFIED SOUNDS, OR FOR CHORD CHANGE SPEED BUILDING. 3-NOTE TRIADS ARE VERY POPULAR WITH GUITARIST AND ARE PLAYED THREE (3) WAYS: WHEN THE ROOT NOTE IS PLAYED ON THE THICKEST STRING, THIS IS KNOWN AS THE ROOT POSITION. NEXT IS THE FIRST (1ST) INVERSION, WHERE THE ROOT NOTE IS PLAYED ON THE THINNEST STRING. FINALLY, THE SECOND (2ND) INVERSION IS WHERE THE ROOT NOTE IS THE MIDDLE STRING OF A TRIAD (3 NOTE) CHORD.

PLAY @ FRET / CHORD
  5   - Am - R
  10 - Dm - R
  12 - Em - R

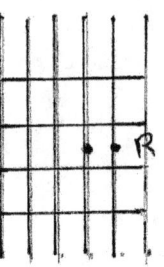

PLAY @ FRET / CHORD
  8   - C MAJ - R
  13 (1) - F MAJ - R
  15 (3) - G MAJ - R

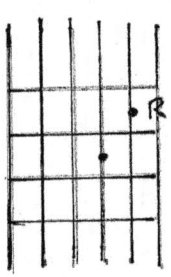

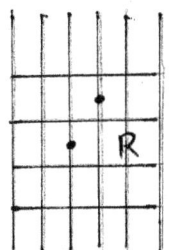

FRET / CHORD

10 - Am - R
3 (15) - Dm - R
5 (17) - Em - R

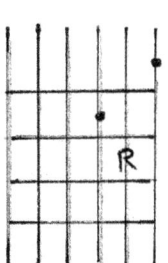

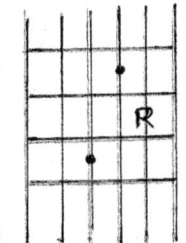

FRET / CHORD

1 (13) - Cmaj - R
6 - Fmaj - R
8 - Gmaj - R

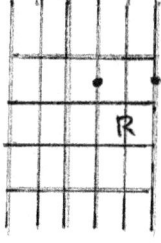

FRET / CHORD
2(14) - Am - R
7 - Dm - R
9 - Em - R

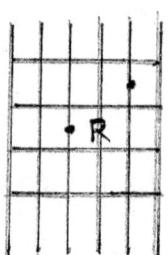

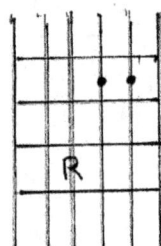

FRET / CHORD
7 - Am - R
12 - Dm - R
14 - Em - R

FRET / CHORD
5 - Cmaj - R
10 - Fmaj - R
12 - Gmaj - R

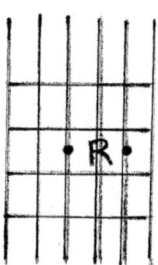

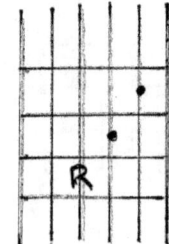

FRET / CHORD
10 - Cmaj - R
3 - Fmaj - R
5 - Gmaj - R

INTERVALS: THE DISTANCE BETWEEN ANY TWO NOTES IS AN INTERVAL. INTERVALS ARE EITHER MELODIC FOR NOTES OR HARMONIC FOR CHORDS. STARTING WITH ANY SINGLE NOTE, ALSO CALLED ROOT FOR CHORDS OR TONIC FOR SCALES, MELODIC SCALE STEPS OCCUR. MAJOR SCALES AND MINOR SCALES EACH HAVE THEIR OWN SCALE STEPS. SCALE STEPS CAN BE DEFINED AS FRET DISTANCES BETWEEN THE NOTES OF A SCALE. SCALE STEPS START WITH THE FIRST LETTER NAME, CALLED THE TONIC. THE DISTANCE (HALF STEP OR WHOLE STEP) BETWEEN THE TONIC AND THE NEXT LETTER (SECOND LETTER) IS THE FIRST (1ST) SCALE STEP. SCALE STEPS CONTINUE TO BE BUILT IN THIS MANNER. THE DISTANCE (HALF STEP OR WHOLE STEP) BETWEEN THE SECOND LETTER OF A SCALE AND THE THIRD LETTER OF A SCALE IS THE SECOND (2ND) SCALE STEP. THIS MANNER OF PROCESS CONTINUES THROUGH THE ENTIRE SCALE. THE FRET DISTANCE BETWEEN EVERY LETTER (NOTE) IN A SCALE IS A SCALE STEP. NOTE: THE PENTATONIC SCALE (5 NOTE SCALE) WILL CONTAIN SCALE STEPS OF ONE AND A HALF (1½) WHOLE STEPS (3 FRETS). IN MUSIC, EVERY SCALE HAS DEFINED STEPS (FORMULA). EXAMPE: C MAJOR USES THE MAJOR SCALE. A MINOR USES THE MINOR SCALE. C MAJOR AND A MINOR EACH HAVE THEIR OWN SCALE STEPS (FORMULA). ALSO, C MAJOR AND A MINOR ARE RELATIVE SCALES: THEY SHARE THE EXACT SAME NOTES. THE DIFFERENCE? THE STARTING POINT (TONIC). C STARTS AT C NOTE, A STARTS AT A NOTE, USING EXACT SAME SCALE (NOTES). SUGGESTION: STUDY THE SCALE STEPS OF EACH SCALE AND DOUBLE CHECK FRET DISTANCES (USE GUITAR NECK PICTURE GRID). REMEMBER, C STARTS AT C NOTE (C, D, E, F, G, A, B). A STARTS AT A NOTE (A, B, C, D, E, F, G). THE FRET DISTANCES BETWEEN THE NOTES ARE THE SCALE STEPS (INERVAL).

INTERVALS: THE DISTANCE BETWEEN ANY TWO NOTES IS AN INTERVAL. INTERVALS ARE EITHER MELODIC FOR NOTES OR HARMONIC FOR CHORDS. STARTING WITH ANY SINGLE NOTE, ALSO CALLED TONIC FOR SCALES OR ROOT FOR CHORDS, COUNTING FRETS ONE AT A TIME (SEMI-TONES, HALF-STEPS) WILL GIVE HARMONIC CHORD NAME.

THE SEVEN (7) NOTE SCALE (C MAJOR, A MINOR) IS CONSIDERED DIATONIC. A DIATONIC SCALE IS A SEVEN NOTE SCALE CONTAINING FIVE (5) WHOLE STEPS AND TWO (2) HALF STEPS. ALL THE NOTES IN A DIATONIC SCALE WILL CONTAIN ALL THE NOTES USED IN DIATONIC CHORDS. DIATONIC CHORDS (ALL CHORDS STUDIED UP TO NOW) CONTAIN ONLY THE SEVEN (7) NOTES FOUND WITHIN THE DIATONIC SCALE. HOWEVER, WITHIN THE DIATONIC SCALE, IF ALL THE HALF (½) STEPS (THE FRETS BETWEEN THE NOTES) WERE FILLED IN WITH FLAT (b) NOTES OR SHARP (#) NOTES, A NEW SCALE WILL OCCUR: THE CHROMATIC SCALE. THE CHROMATIC SCALE CONTAINS TWELVE (12) NOTES AND HAS THE EXTENED NOTES (FLATS AND SHARPS) NEEDED TO BUILD ON THE TRIAD (3-NOTE) CHORDS THAT HAVE BEEN STUDIED UP TO NOW.

(7) SEVEN NOTES (DIATONIC)

INTERVAL	SCALE DEGREE
C – PERFECT UNISON (TONIC)	C – TONIC
D – MAJOR SECOND (2ND)	D – SUPERTONIC
E – MAJOR THIRD (3RD)	E – MEDIANT
F – PERFECT FOURTH (4TH)	F – SUBDOMINANT
G – PERFECT FIFTH (5TH)	G – DOMINANT
A – MAJOR SIXTH (6TH)	A – SUBMEDIANT
B – MAJOR SEVENTH (MAJ 7TH)	B – LEADING TONE

CHROMATIC SCALE (INTERVALS)

			(FRET DISTANCE)
TONIC	-	C	- 0
MINOR 2ND	-	D^b	- 1
MAJOR 2ND	-	D	- 2
MINOR 3RD	-	E^b	- 3
MAJOR 3RD	-	E	- 4
PERFECT 4TH	-	F	- 5
* TRITONE	-	$F^\#/G^b$	- 6
PERFECT 5TH	-	G	- 7
MINOR 6TH	-	A^b	- 8
MAJOR 6TH	-	A	- 9
MINOR 7TH	-	B^b	- 10
MAJOR 7TH	-	B	- 11
OCTIVE	-	C	- 12

* NOTE: TRITONE - 3 TONES (WHOLE STEPS) BETWEEN TONIC AND OCTIVE

C MAJOR / A MINOR SCALE NOTES:

```
C  D  E  F  G  A  B
1  2  3  4  5  6  7
A  B  C  D  E  F  G
```

MAJOR SCALE STEPS : START @ C NOTE (TONIC)

1 - 1 - ½ - 1 - 1 - 1 - ½ (STEPS)
C D E F G A B C

MINOR SCALE STEPS : START @ A NOTE (TONIC)

1 - ½ - 1 - 1 - ½ - 1 - 1 (STEPS)
A B C D E F G A

MAJOR CHORD : 2 STEPS TO 3RD

START @ C NOTE : C, E, G - C MAJOR
START @ F NOTE : F, A, C - F MAJOR
START @ G NOTE : G, B, D - G MAJOR

MINOR CHORD : 1 ½ STEPS TO 3RD

START @ A NOTE : A, C, E - A MINOR
START @ D NOTE : D, F, A - D MINOR
START @ E NOTE : E, G, B - E MINOR

NOTE:

FIRST LETTER OF CHORD BECOMES ROOT
SECOND LETTER OF MAJOR CHORD IS MAJOR 3RD (FRET DISTANCE: 4)
SECOND LETTER OF MINOR CHORD IS MINOR 3RD (FRET DISTANCE: 3)
THIRD LETTER OF CHORD IS PERFECT 5TH (FRET DISTANCE: 7)

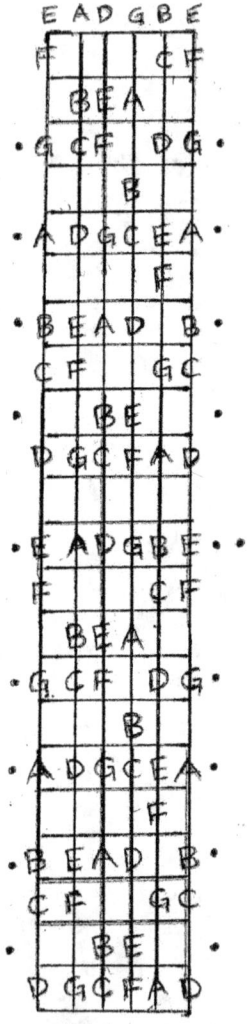

ROMAN NUMERALS ARE A FORM OF WRITTEN NOTATION USED TO IDENTIFY CHORDS WITHIN A CHORD PROGRESSION. EXAMPLE: KEY OF C MAJOR —

C MAJOR, D MINOR, E MINOR, F MAJOR, G MAJOR, A MINOR, B DIMINISHED
   I   ii   iii   IV   V   vi   vii°

MAJOR CHORDS ARE UPPER CASE ROMAN NUMERALS. MINOR CHORDS ARE LOWER CASE ROMAN NUMERALS. SOMETIMES, UPPER CASE ROMAN NUMERALS ARE USED FOR ALL CHORDS, WHEREIN NEXT TO AN UPPER CASE NUMERAL, A LOWER CASE LETTER m IS PLACED TO INDICATE A MINOR CHORD.

RELATIVE CHORDS:
C MAJOR RELATIVE A MINOR
F MAJOR RELATIVE D MINOR
G MAJOR RELATIVE E MINOR

ALL MAJOR CHORDS SHARE TWO (2) NOTES WITH THEIR RELATIVE MINOR CHORDS. THE MAJOR CHORD ROOT NOTE IS THE MINOR CHORD'S MINOR THIRD (3RD) NOTE. THE MAJOR CHORD'S MAJOR THIRD (3RD) NOTE IS THE MINOR CHORD'S PERFECT FIFTH (5TH) NOTE.

THE C MAJOR AND A MINOR ARE BOTH CHORDS THAT SHARE THE NOTES: C AND E
THE F MAJOR AND D MINOR ARE BOTH CHORDS THAT SHARE THE NOTES: F AND A
THE G MAJOR AND E MINOR ARE BOTH CHORDS THAT SHARE THE NOTES: G AND B
IN CHORD PROGRESSIONS, SINCE THEY SHARE THE SAME TWO (2) NOTES, MAJOR CHORDS CAN BE SUBSTITUTED WITH THEIR RELATIVE MINOR CHORDS. THIS SUBSTITUTION GIVES THE CHORD PROGRESSION A SLIGHTLY DIFFERENT, DARKER FEEL.

MUSIC SCALES AND MODES

SCALES AND MODES ARE BOTH SETS OF NOTES. SCALES AND MODES ARE SIMILAR IN THAT BOTH ARE STUDIED AND PLAYED AS NOTE PATTERNS ON THE GUITAR NECK. THIS PATTERN WILL FORM AN EASILY IDENTIFIED SHAPE THAT CAN BE MOVED ALONG THE GUITAR NECK TO ANY FRET OF A DESIRED LETTER NAME (TONIC). SCALES AND MODES ARE ALSO SIMILAR IN THAT THEY BOTH CAN BE PLAYED IN TWO WAYS: EITHER AS PART OF THE RHYTHM SOUND OR AS THE LEAD SOUND. IN ADDITION, SCALES AND MODES ARE ALSO SIMILAR IN THAT THEY BOTH STAND ALONE! THE NOTES OF EACH SCALE OR MODE ARE PLAYED USING THE TONIC NOTE THAT CHANGES ALONG WITH THE CHANGES OF THE CHORD PROGRESSION. AS THE CHORDS IN THE CHORD PROGRESSION CHANGE, THE ROOT LETTER OF THE NEWLY CHANGED CHORD IS USED AS THE BASIS FOR THE TONIC LETTER OF A SCALE OR MODE. THUS, THE SCALE OR MODE FOLLOWS (CHASES) THE CHORD PROGRESSION.

MODES DIFFER FROM SCALES IN THAT UNLIKE SCALE NOTES, THE NOTES OF MODES BELONG TO A SET OF MODES THAT ALL SHARE THE EXACT SAME (7) SEVEN NOTES. IN THIS SET OF MODES, THERE ARE SEVEN MODE SHAPES. THE (7) SEVEN NOTES, WHICH ARE DIATONIC, ARE EACH THE STARTING POINT (TONIC) OF EACH MODE SHAPE. USING THE SAME (7) SEVEN NOTES, ONLY THE STARTING POINT (TONIC) CHANGES POSITIONS. THE NOTES HOLD THEIR POSITIONS WHILE THE TONIC MOVES TO THE NEXT NOTE.

THE SEVEN MODE NAMES, IN THE CORRECT ORDER, ARE: IONIAN (I), DORIAN (ii), PHRYGIAN (iii), LYDIAN (IV), MIXOLYDIAN (V), AEOLIAN (vi), LOCRIAN (vii°). MAJOR MODES ARE IONIAN, LYDIAN, MIXOLYDIAN. MINOR MODES ARE AEOLIAN, DORIAN, PHRYGIAN. THE SEVENTH MODE, LOCRIAN IS A DIMINISHED MODE. SIX MODES PAIR WELL TOGETHER: IONIAN WITH AEOLIAN, LYDIAN WITH DORIAN, MIXOLYDIAN WITH PHRYGIAN. THE SEVENTH MODE, LOCRIAN (SINCE IT SHARES THE SAME NOTES) WORKS WELL AS A FILLER MODE ALONG THE GUITAR NECK.

Each mode has it's own shape on the guitar neck. However, for practical purposes, learning just three of the modes, the minor modes, will be easier than trying to learn all the modes all at once. Found within these minor modes, there will be their paired (relative) major mode notes. Both modes can be found within the same mode shape. Just start with the tonic note that matches the root note of the chord. Major tonic with major root, minor tonic with minor root. Also, there is a pentatonic (5 note) scale found within each mode. This pentatonic scale is both major and minor depending on which tonic note is used to start. This is a very useful scale with a very clean sound. In addition, there is a blues note (looks like this O) added to the pentatonic scale. This added note turns the pentatonic scale into a blues scale. The same blues note is added to the aeolian mode. This added note turns the aeolian mode into a minor blues scale. By the way, this blues note is a flattened fifth note (5^b). (3^b) for major pentatonic.

Now, the actual letter note and fret positions of the modes. Modes are defined starting with the Ionian mode, it is the first mode of any set of modes. The Ionian mode has the exact same notes as a major scale. Staying with C major scale notes C, D, E, F, G, A, B (no flats, no sharps) each mode is as follows: C-Ionian, D-Dorian, E-Phrygian, F-Lydian, G-Mixolydian, A-Aeolian, B-Locrian.

Now on the guitar fret board:
A @ 5th fret, C @ 8th fret / D @ 10th fret, F @ 13th fret / E @ 12th fret, G @ 15th fret

Pairs once more: A-Aeolian, C Ionian / D-Dorian, F-Lydian / E-Phrygian, G-Mixolydian

Notice how the pairs of modes are same as the pairs of relative chords:
A minor with C major / D minor with F major / E minor with G major.

Thus, the pairs of modes are relative modes.

In addition, the notes of the B-Locrian mode are found on the guitar neck between the 7th fret and the 10th fret and make a nice fill pattern between the A minor (Aeolian) and D minor (Dorian) modes.

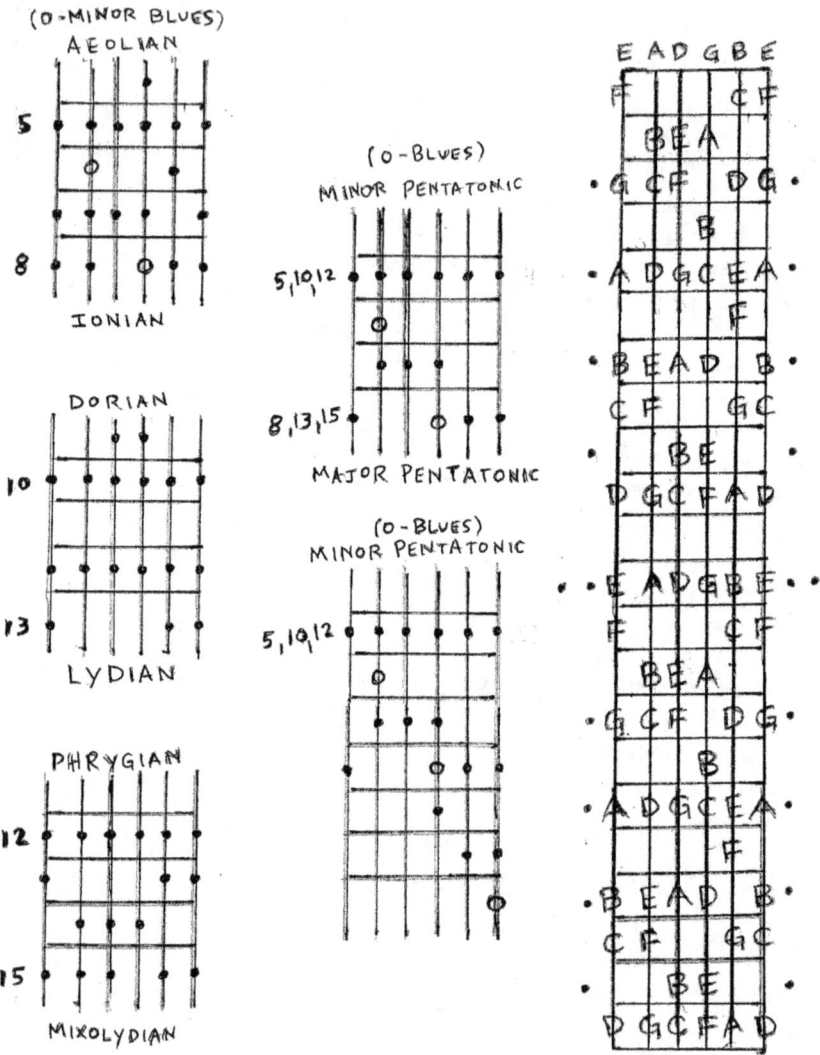

STRING (NOTE) BENDING

SCALE AND MODE NOTE PITCH (HZ) CAN BE PHYSICALLY ALTERED. THE IDEA OF BENDING NOTES IS THAT OF LETTING A NOTE RING, THEN PHYSICALLY USING YOUR FINGER(S) TO PUSH OR PULL A GUITAR STRING ALONG A FRET. THE GUITAR STRING STAYS IN CONTACT WITH THE FRET. THIS PHYSICAL ACTION STRETCHES THE GUITAR STRING, CAUSING THE PITCH (HZ) TO RAISE. PRE-BENDING IS STRETCHING A GUITAR STRING PRIOR TO (BEFORE) A NOTE BEING RUNG. WHEN IT COMES TO NOTE BENDING, ANY STRING (NOTE) CAN BE BENT. HOWEVER, THE MOST USEFUL STRING BENDS ARE THE ONES THAT MAKE THE MOST SENSE: BENDING THE MINOR 3RD ONE HALF (½) STEP TO THE MAJOR 3RD, BENDING THE PERFECT 4TH ONE WHOLE (W) STEP TO THE PERFECT 5TH AND BENDING THE MINOR 7TH (b7) ONE WHOLE (W) TO THE OCTIVE (ROOT) OR THE MAJOR 7TH (MAJ 7TH) ONE HALF (½) STEP TO THE OCTIVE (ROOT). STRONG SOUNDING NOTES ARE REACHED USING LESSER STRENGTH NOTES AND RAISING THEIR PITCH (HZ).

EXERCISE: DURING PRACTICE SESSIONS, CHECK THE PITCH (HZ) SOUNDS: ONE HALF (½) STEP - 1 FRET, ONE WHOLE (W) STEP - 2 FRETS. THE SOUND OF THE BENT NOTE SHOULD SOUND THE SAME AS THE NOTE ONE OR TWO FRETS HIGHER. GUITAR BENDS ARE GREAT SOUND TECHNIQUE.

EXTENDED CHORDS

EXTENDED CHORDS ARE THE ADDITION OF NOTES TO THE THREE NOTE (TRIAD) CHORDS. THESE CAN BE MORE OF THE SAME NOTES (TRIAD), CREATING A MORE RICH SOUND, OR NEW NOTES CAN BE ADDED (USING CHROMATIC SCALE) TO CREATE NEW CHARACTERISTICS ON TOP OF TRIAD CHORDS. EXAMPLES ARE: MAJOR - C6, C7, C9 OR MINOR - Amb, Am7, Am9.

FRET / CHORD
8 — CMAJ — R
1(13) — FMAJ — R
3(15) — GMAJ — R

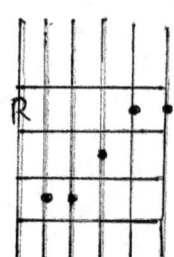

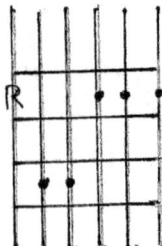

FRET / CHORD
5 — Am — R
10 — Dm — R
12 — Em — R

FRET / CHORD
3(15) — CMAJ — R
8 — FMAJ — R
10 — GMAJ — R

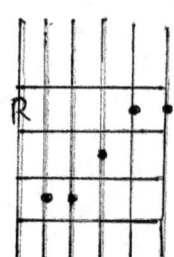

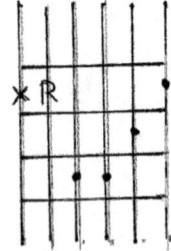

FRET / CHORD
12 — Am — R
5 — Dm — R
7 — Em — R

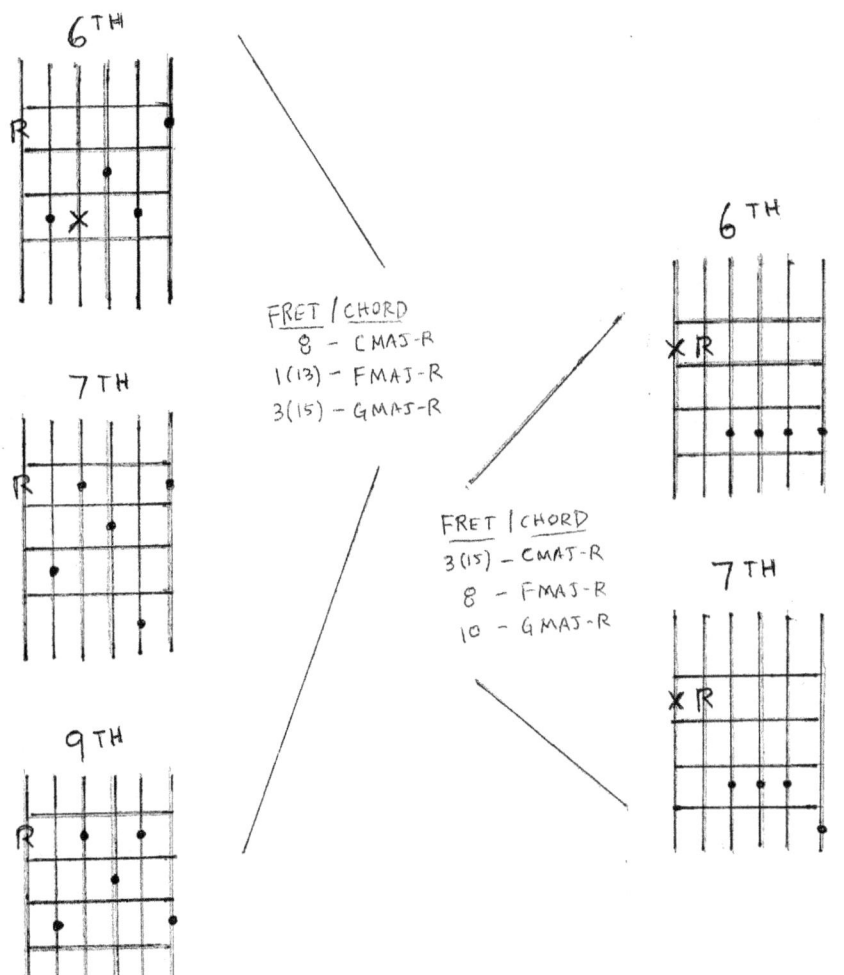

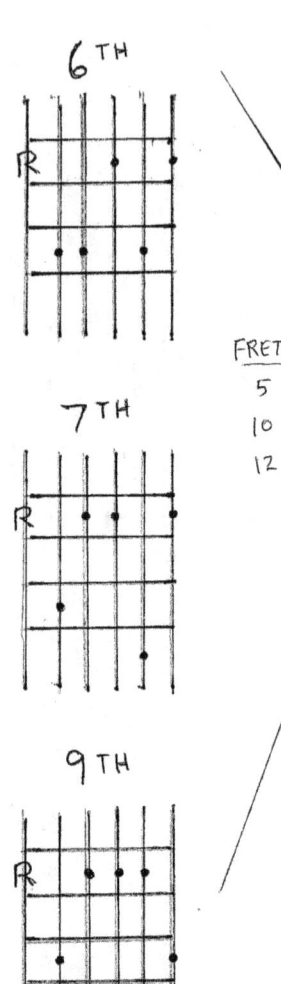
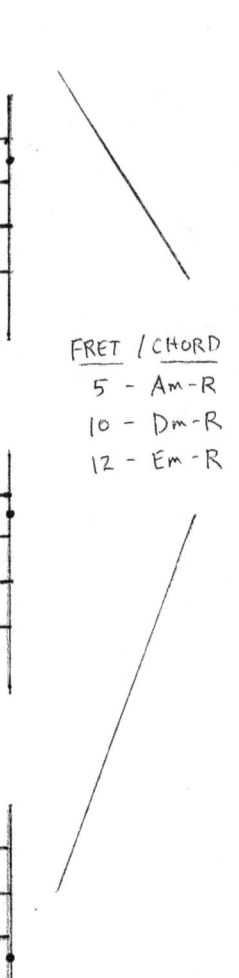

FRET / CHORD
5 - Am - R
10 - Dm - R
12 - Em - R

FRET / CHORD
12 - Am - R
5 - Dm - R
7 - Em - R

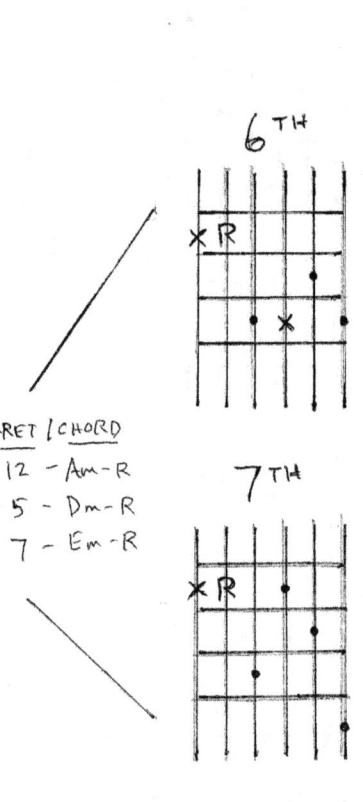

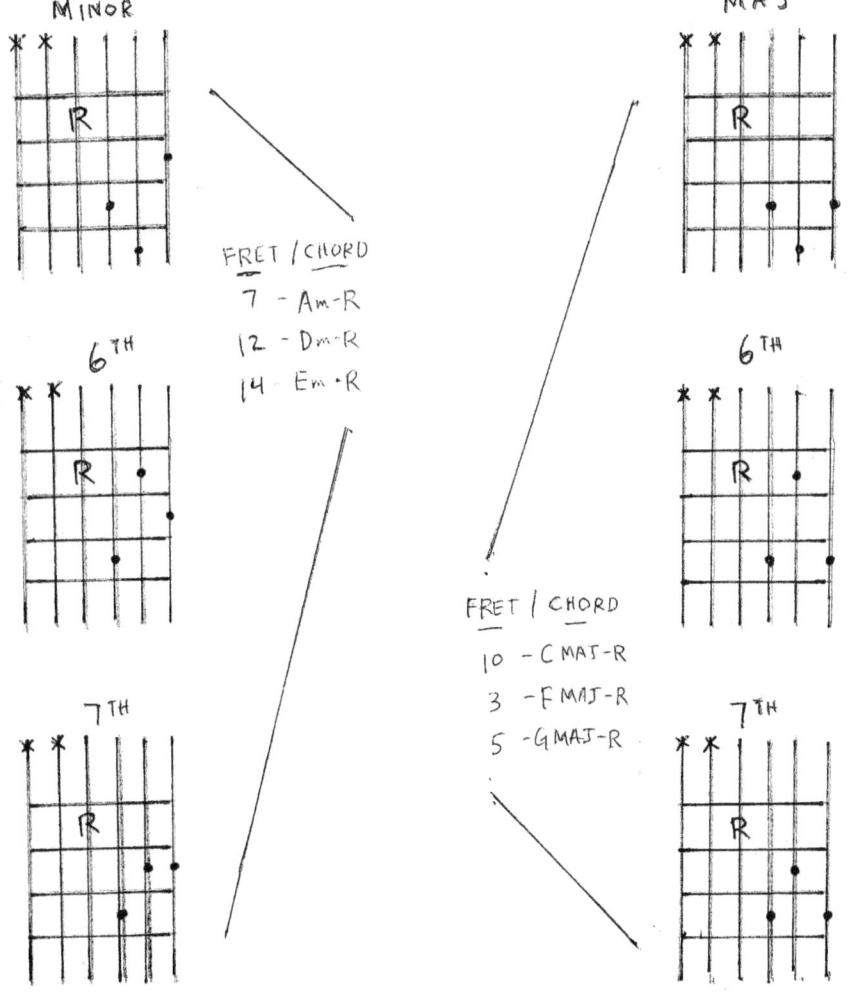

EXTENDED CHORD PROGRESSIONS

(DORIAN) — $Am6$, $Dm6$, $Em6$
$1-\frac{1}{2}-1-1-1-\frac{1}{2}-1$ i   iv   v

(MINOR BLUES) — $Am7$, $Dm7$, $Em7$
$1-\frac{1}{2}-1-\frac{1}{2}-\frac{1}{2}-\frac{1}{2}-1-1$ i   iv   v

(MIXOLYDIAN) — C^7, F^7, G^7
$1-1-\frac{1}{2}-1-1-\frac{1}{2}-1$ I   IV   V

(MAJOR PENTATONIC) — C^6, F^6, G^6
$1-1-1\frac{1}{2}-1-1\frac{1}{2}$ I   IV   V

(MINOR PENTATONIC) — Am, Dm, Em
$1\frac{1}{2}-1-1-1\frac{1}{2}-1$ i   iv   v
                         A^7, D^7, E^7
                         I   IV   V

(BLUES) — $C7$, $F7$, $G7$
$1\frac{1}{2}-1-\frac{1}{2}-\frac{1}{2}-1\frac{1}{2}-1$ I   IV   V

THESE LAST TWO SCALES CAN BE PLAYED FROM THE I (i) POSITION OVER ALL THREE CHORDS. NOTICE, WITH THE MINOR PENTATONIC, MINOR CHORD PROGRESSIONS OR 7TH CHORD PROGRESSIONS (MAJOR CHORDS W/b7) PLAY. BOTH PROGRESSIONS CAN BE PLAYED WITH THE MINOR PENTATONIC.

ALSO, THE FIRST FOUR SCALES ARE CONSIDERED CHORD CHASERS. THE SCALE FOLLOWS THE LETTER NAME OF EACH CHORD IN A PROGRESSION; PHYSICALLY MOVING SCALE SHAPE TO NEW CHORD LETTER NAME LOCATION. FRET LETTER NAME IS LOCATED ON THE E STRING.

MORE MODE THEORY (SCALES)

WHEN PLAYING SCALES OR MODES AS PART OF THE RHYTHM, NOTES CAN BE PART OF THE MELODY OF THE BASS GUITAR, PART OF THE STRUM PATTERN OR LICK PATTERN OF THE RHYTHM GUITAR, OR PART OF THE BEATS PATTERN OF PERCUSSION (DRUMS). HOWEVER, AS MUCH AS THIS IS A GREAT RHYTHM SOUND, SCALES AND MODES SOUND THEIR GREATEST AS A LEAD SOUND. LEAD SOLOS RISE ABOVE THE REST OF THE MUSIC AND ARE PERFECT FOR BRIDGING BETWEEN A SONG'S CHORUS AND TAKING AN AUDIO SCENIC ROUTE BACK TO THE SONG'S VERSE.

WHEN PLAYING A SCALE OR MODE SOLO OVER A CHORD PROGRESSION, MOST IMPORTANT IS PLAYING THE SAME LETTER NOTE (TONIC) AT THE EXACT SAME TIME AS THE CHORD ROOT ENTERS THE PROGRESSION. THE BASS GUITAR AND THE RHYTHM GUITAR ARE TOGETHER PLAYING THE SAME LETTER NOTE (CHORD ROOT) THROUGH THE ENTIRE PROGRESSION. WHEN THEY CHANGE CHORDS, THE LEAD GUITAR ALSO NEEDS TO CHANGE CHORDS WITH THEM. AS A SOLOIST, BUILDING UP TO THE CHORD CHANGE, PASSING NOTES ARE USED. PASSING NOTES, OR PASSING TONES AS THEY'RE SOMETIMES CALLED, ARE THE OTHER NOTES WITHIN A SCALE OR MODE THAT ARE NOT ANY OF THE NOTES OF THE CHORD. SOME PASSING NOTES SOUND BETTER (THE DISSONANT ONES) THAN OTHERS. WHAT'S BEST IS TO SOUND OUT WHAT YOU LIKE OR WHAT YOU THINK SOUNDS BEST. REMEMBER, BUILDING UP TO A CHORD CHANGE, YOU ARE STILL PLAYING WITHIN (PLAYING OVER) A CHORD. THE PARTICULAR CHORD YOU'RE PLAYING WITHIN (PLAYING OVER) MUST BE TAKEN INTO CONSIDERATION. YOU ENTER A CHORD (BEGINNING OF MEASURE) WITH CHORD NOTES IN MIND. YOU EXIT A CHORD (ENDING OF MEASURE) WITH PASSING NOTES IN MIND. WHILE PLAYING TOWARDS THE NEXT CHORD (CHORD CHANGE) AND WHILE STAYING WITHIN A SCALE OR MODE, THINK ABOUT ALL THE NOTES: THE CHORD NOTES AND THE BUILD UP NOTES (PASSING TONES).

ALSO, BESIDES PASSING TONES, THERE ARE WHAT'S CALLED ARPEGGIOS. THESE ARE THE EXACT NOTES OF THE CHORDS YOU'RE PLAYING WITHIN (OVER). ARPEGGIOS CAN BE IN THE FORM OF SCALES, OR SCALE PATTERNS FOUND WITHIN MODE PATTERNS. ARPEGGIOS HAVE A UNIQUE SOUND. AGAIN, SOUND OUT WHAT YOU LIKE AND WHAT YOU LIKE BEST. THIS IS YOUR SOLO! IF YOU LIKE COMBINING (MIXING) PASSING TONES AND CHORD TONES (ARPEGGIOS) THEN THAT'S WHAT YOU LIKE.

MODES : THEORY

THE NOTES OF ANY SET OF MODES WILL ALL BE THE SAME. EACH INDIVIDUAL MODE SHARE THE EXACT SAME NOTES AS EVERY OTHER MODE IN A GIVEN SET OF MODES.

IONIAN - C D E F G A B
        I ii iii IV V vi vii°
        W - W - ½ - W - W - W - ½

   DORIAN - D E F G A B C
           i ii III IV v vi° VII
           W - ½ - W - W - W - ½ - W

      PHRYGIAN - E F G A B C D
              i II III iv v° VI vii
              ½ - W - W - W - ½ - W - W

         LYDIAN - F G A B C D E
                I II iii iv° V vi vii
                W - W - W - ½ - W - W - ½

           MIXOLYDIAN - G A B C D E F
                    I ii iii° IV v vi VII
                    W - W - ½ - W - W - ½ - W

              AEOLIAN - A B C D E F G
                      i ii III iv v VI VII
                      W - ½ - W - W - ½ - W - W

                 LOCRIAN - B C D E F G A
                          i II iii iv V VI vii
                          ½ - W - W - ½ - W - W - W

THE STARTING NOTE (TONIC) CHANGES TO THE LETTER NAME OF THE NEW MODE. THE FIRST NOTE IS THE LETTER NAME OF THE NEW MODE : C - IONIAN, D - DORIAN, E - PHRYGIAN, F - LYDIAN, G - MIXOLYDIAN, A - AEOLIAN, B - LOCRIAN. THE LETTER NAME BECOMES THE NEW TONIC OF THE NEW SCALE AND THE NEW ROOT OF THE CHORD PROGRESSION. ALL THE NOTES IN ALL THE

MODES ARE EXACTLY THE SAME. THE DIFFERENCE IS THE CHORDS! THE CHORD PROGRESSIONS ARE BUILT ON THE LETTER NAMES OF THE NEW TONIC OF EACH MODE. CHORDS ARE HEARD THE MOST! IN MUSIC, AS MUCH AS THE NOTES ARE HEARD WHEN PLAYED, CHORDS ARE HEARD EVEN MORE! IN ADDITION TO PLAYING CHORD PROGRESSIONS BUILT ON THE NEW MODE, ALSO PLAY THE NOTES OF THE NEW TONIC OF THE NEW MODE, ALOT. ALSO PLAY ALOT THE CHARACTERISTICS ASSOCIATED WITH THE NEW MODE: USING SCALE STEPS, MODE CHARACTERISTICS (EASILY CHECKED USING CHROMATIC SCALE):

I - IONIAN - NO FLATS / NO SHARPS → (MAJOR SCALE) NO CHARACTERISTICS
ii - DORIAN - b3, b7 → MAJOR 6TH
iii - PHRYGIAN - b2, b3, b6, b7 → MINOR 2ND
IV - LYDIAN - #4 → RAISED 4TH (TRITONE)
V - MIXOLYDIAN - b7 → MINOR 7TH
vi - AEOLIAN - b3, b6, b7 → MINOR 6TH (NATURAL MINOR SCALE)
vii - LOCRIAN - b2, b3, b5, b6, b7 → LOWERED 5TH (TRITONE)

3-MAJOR MODES: IONIAN, LYDIAN, MIXOLYDIAN.   1 - DIMINISHED
3-MINOR MODES: AEOLIAN, DORIAN, PHRYGIAN →   MODE: LOCRIAN

NOTES: MAJOR MODES HAVE MAJOR 3RDS, MINOR MODES HAVE MINOR 3RDS (b3)

NOTES: DORIAN MODE HAS MAJOR 6TH,
    AEOLIAN AND PHRYGIAN BOTH HAVE MINOR 6TH (b6)

NOTES: LYDIAN MODE HAS A SHARP 4TH (#4) (RAISED 4TH),
    IONIAN AND MIXOLYDIAN BOTH HAVE PERFECT 4THS (NOT MINOR, NOT MAJOR)

NOTES: MIXOLYDIAN MODE HAS MINOR 7TH (b7)
    IONIAN AND LYDIAN BOTH HAVE MAJOR 7TH (MAJ 7TH)

NOTES: LOCRIAN MODE HAS DIMINISHED (FLATTENED) 5TH (b5), ALL OTHER
    MODES HAVE PERFECT 5THS (NOT MINOR, NOT MAJOR)

NOTES: LOCRIAN AND PHRYGIAN BOTH HAVE MINOR 2ND (b2)

MODAL CHORD PROGRESSIONS

C (IONIAN) — C, F, G7 ; C, Dm, G
1-1-½-1-1-1-½   I IV V7   I ii V

D (DORIAN) — Dm, Em, G ; Dm, C, G7
1-½-1-1-1-½-1   i ii IV   i VII IV7

E (Phrygian) — Em, F, Dm
½-1-1-1-½-1-1   i II vii

F (Lydian) — F, G
1-1-1-½-1-1-½   I II

G (MIXOLYDIAN) — G, F, C ; G, Dm, F
1-1-½-1-1-½-1   I VII IV   I v VII

A (AEOLIAN) — Am, Dm, Em ; Am, F, G
1-½-1-1-½-1-1   i iv v   i VI VII

THESE SIX MODES ARE USUALLY PLAYED FROM ONE SCALE POSITION: THE I (i) POSITION. HOWEVER, ANY OF THE NOTES FROM THE SCALE CAN BE PLAYED AT ANY FRET THEY APPEAR. THIS IS HELPFUL WHEN THERE IS A NEED TO KEEP SCALE NOTES CLOSE TO CHORDS ALONG THE GUITAR NECK.

ALSO, THERE IS A SEVENTH MODE: B (LOCRIAN). PURPOSELY LEFT OUT DUE TO LACK OF SOUND RESOLVE (½-1-1-½-1-1-1). NOTICE THE INTERVAL BETWEEN THE 4TH AND 5TH NOTE IS ½ STEP. THIS CREATES A FLATTENED FIFTH (b5) NOTE: (DIMISHED CHORD).

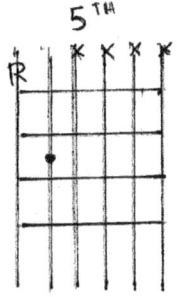 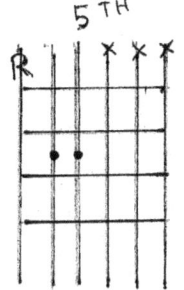 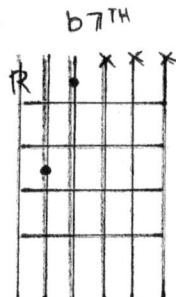

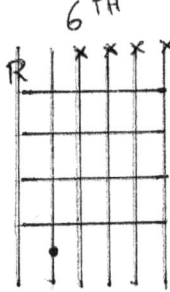

FRET / CHORD
5 - A
8 - C
10 - D
12 - E
(1)13 - F
(3)15 - G

POWER CHORDS

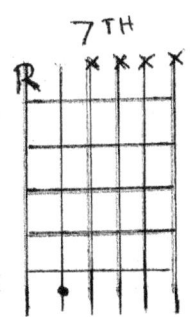

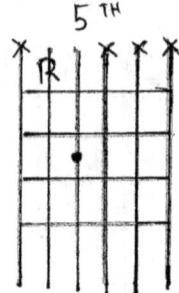
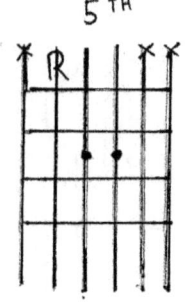
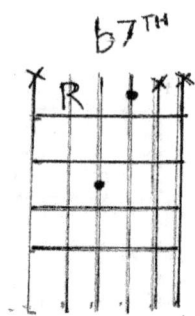

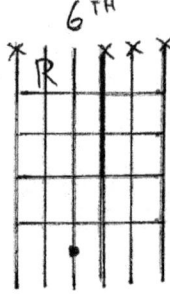

FRET	CHORD
(15) 3	— C
5	— D
7	— E
8	— F
10	— G
12	— A

POWER CHORDS

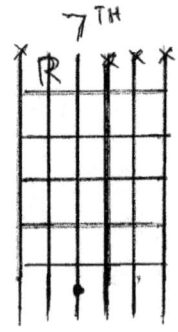

POWER CHORD - ROCK N ROLL - 8 BAR BLUES

TWO (2) WAYS TO LEARN: FOUR (4) DOWN STRUMS OR EIGHT (8) DOWN STRUMS. STAY WITH C, F, G CHORDS TOGETHER OR A, D, E CHORDS TOGETHER AS PROGRESSIONS (LATER, YOU CAN MIX ALL CHORDS IN PROGRESSIONS).

1. - FOUR DOWN STRUMS - @ C CHORD (OR A CHORD)
   1ST AND 2ND STRUM IS 5TH CHORD, 3RD STRUM IS 6TH CHORD, 4TH STRUM IS 5TH CHORD. PLAY THIS FOUR DOWN STRUMS FOUR (4) TIMES.

   - FOUR DOWN STRUMS - @ F CHORD (OR D CHORD)
   1ST AND 2ND STRUM IS 5TH CHORD, 3RD STRUM IS 6TH CHORD, 4TH STRUM IS 5TH CHORD. PLAY THIS FOUR DOWN STRUMS TWO (2) TIMES.

   - FOUR DOWN STRUMS - @ G CHORD (OR E CHORD)
   1ST AND 2ND STRUM IS 5TH CHORD, 3RD STRUM IS 6TH CHORD, 4TH STRUM IS 5TH CHORD. PLAY THIS FOUR DOWN STRUMS ONE (1) TIME.

   - FOUR DOWN STRUMS - @ C CHORD (OR A CHORD)
   1ST AND 2ND STRUM IS 5TH CHORD, 3RD STRUM IS 6TH CHORD, 4TH STRUM IS 5TH CHORD. PLAY THIS FOUR DOWN STRUMS ONE (1) TIME.

2. - EIGHT DOWN STRUMS - @ C CHORD (OR A CHORD)
   1ST AND 2ND STRUM IS 5TH CHORD, 3RD STRUM IS 6TH CHORD, 4TH STRUM IS 5TH CHORD, 5TH STRUM IS 7TH CHORD, 6TH STRUM IS 5TH CHORD, 7TH STRUM IS 6TH CHORD, 8TH STRUM IS 5TH CHORD. PLAY THIS EIGHT DOWN STRUMS FOUR (4) TIMES.

- EIGHT DOWN STRUMS - @ F CHORD (OR D CHORD)
  1ST AND 2ND STRUM IS 5TH CHORD, 3RD STRUM IS 6TH CHORD, 4TH STRUM IS 5TH CHORD, 5TH STRUM IS 7TH CHORD, 6TH STRUM IS 5TH CHORD, 7TH STRUM IS 6TH CHORD, 8TH STRUM IS 5TH CHORD. PLAY THIS EIGHT DOWN STRUMS TWO (2) TIMES.

- EIGHT DOWN STRUMS - @ G CHORD (OR E CHORD)
  1ST AND 2ND STRUM IS 5TH CHORD, 3RD STRUM IS 6TH CHORD, 4TH STRUM IS 5TH CHORD, 5TH STRUM IS 7TH CHORD, 6TH STRUM IS 5TH CHORD, 7TH STRUM IS 6TH CHORD, 8TH STRUM IS 5TH CHORD. PLAY THIS EIGHT DOWN STRUMS ONE (1) TIME.

- EIGHT DOWN STRUMS - @ C CHORD (OR A CHORD)
  1ST AND 2ND STRUM IS 5TH CHORD, 3RD STRUM IS 6TH CHORD, 4TH STRUM IS 5TH CHORD, 5TH STRUM IS 7TH CHORD, 6TH STRUM IS 5TH CHORD, 7TH STRUM IS 6TH CHORD, 8TH STRUM IS 5TH CHORD. PLAY THIS EIGHT DOWN STRUMS ONE (1) TIME.

* NOTE: A POWER CHORD IS A TWO (2) NOTE DYAD CHORD, ALSO KNOWN AS A DOUBLE-STOP. POWER CHORDS CONSIST OF ONLY THE ONE (1) NOTE (ROOT) AND THE FIVE (5) NOTE (PERFECT). THERE ARE NO THIRD (3RD) NOTES. THUS, A POWER CHORD (5TH CHORD) IS NOT A MAJOR CHORD (NO MAJOR 3RD NOTE). A POWER CHORD (5TH CHORD) IS NOT A MINOR CHORD (NO MINOR 3RD NOTE). FOR THIS EXERCISE, THE FIVE (5) NOTE EXTENDS TO A MAJOR 6TH TO BECOME THE SIX (6) NOTE OR THE FIVE (5) NOTE EXTENDS TO A MINOR 7TH TO BECOME THE SEVEN (7) NOTE.

AUGMENTED / DIMINISHED / SUSPENDED CHORDS

AUGMENTED CHORDS, DIMINISHED CHORDS AND SUSPENDED 2/4 CHORDS ARE TRANSITIONAL CHORDS. THEY CREATE A SLIGHT VARIANCE OF SOUND OF EXISTING CHORDS. THIS IS HELPFUL FOR CHORD CHANGES (PROGRESSIONS) AS WELL AS FOR BREAKING UP THE REPETITIVE NATURE OF REPEATED CHORDS LIKE THAT OF SONGS CONTAINING VERSES AND CHORUSES.

THERE ARE THREE TYPES OF AUGMENTED CHORDS: AUGMENTED, AUGMENTED 7TH AND AUGMENTED MAJOR 7TH. ALL CONTAIN A ROOT, MAJOR 3RD, AND SHARP 5 NOTES. AUGMENTED CHORDS ARE NOT MINOR CHORDS (NO MINOR 3RD) AND THEY ARE NOT MAJOR CHORDS (NO PERFECT 5TH). THEY ARE AUGMENTED CHORDS! OF THE THREE TYPES OF AUGMENTED CHORDS, ONLY ONE WILL BE STUDIED BECAUSE ONLY ONE HAS SYMMETRY. THE THREE (3) NOTE AUGMENTED CHORD HAS A SHAPE THAT CAN BE MOVED FOUR (4) FRETS ALONG THE GUITAR NECK AND GIVE THE SAME CHORD WITH THE EXACT SAME SHAPE AND WITH THE EXACT SAME NOTES (THE NOTES ARE REARRANGED). THIS AUGMENTED CHORD IS THE 1, 3, #5 (NOTES) CHORD. TWO OTHER AUGMENTED CHORDS EXIST: THE AUGMENTED 7TH - 1, 3, #5, b7 (NOTES) AND THE AUGMENTED MAJ 7TH - 1, 3, #5, 7 (NOTES). THESE LAST LAST TWO (2) CHORDS DO NOT HAVE THE QUALITY OF SYMMETRY.

THERE ARE THREE TYPES OF DIMINISHED CHORDS: DIMINISHED, HALF DIMINISHED AND DIMINISHED SEVENTH. ALL CONTAIN A ROOT, MINOR 3RD, AND FLAT 5 NOTES. DIMINISHED CHORDS ARE NOT MAJOR CHORDS (NO MAJOR 3RD) AND THEY ARE NOT MINOR CHORDS (NO PERFECT 5TH). THEY ARE DIMINISHED CHORDS! OF THE THREE TYPES OF DIMINISHED CHORDS, ONLY ONE WILL BE STUDIED BECAUSE ONLY ONE HAS SYMMETRY. THE FOUR (4) NOTE DIMINISHED SEVENTH CHORD HAS A SHAPE THAT CAN BE MOVED THREE (3) FRETS

ALONG THE GUITAR NECK AND GIVE THE SAME CHORD WITH THE EXACT SAME SHAPE AND WITH THE EXACT SAME NOTES (THE NOTES ARE REARRANGED). THE DIMINISHED SEVENTH CHORD IS THE 1, b3, b5, bb7 (NOTES) CHORD (THE DOUBLE FLAT SEVENTH (bb7) IS ACTUALLY A MAJOR SIXTH (6), BUT FOR EMPHASIS OF THE SEVENTH NOTE, THE bb IS USED). TWO OTHER DIMINISHED CHORDS EXIST: THE DIMINISHED - 1, b3, b5 (NOTES) AND THE HALF DIMINISHED - 1, b3, b5, b7 (NOTES). THESE LAST TWO (2) CHORDS DO NOT HAVE THE QUALITY OF SYMMETRY.

THERE ARE FOUR TYPES OF SUSPENDED CHORDS: SUS2, 7SUS2, SUS4 AND 7SUS4. ALL CONTAIN A ROOT AND PERFECT 5TH NOTE. SUSPENDED CHORDS ARE NOT MAJOR CHORDS (NO MAJOR 3RD). SUSPENDED CHORDS ARE NOT MINOR CHORDS (NO MINOR 3RD). THEY ARE SUSPENDED CHORDS! OF THE FOUR TYPES OF SUSPENDED CHORDS, TWO WILL BE STUDIED BECAUSE ONLY TWO ARE THREE (3) NOTE CHORDS. THREE (3) NOTES ALLOW FOR SIMPLE CHORD SHAPE CHANGES TO BE OBTAINED. THE SUSPENDED 2 CHORD IS THE 1, 2, 5 (NOTE) CHORD. THE SUSPENDED 4 CHORD IS THE 1, 4, 5 (NOTE) CHORD. NOTICE HOW THE MINOR 3RD NOTE OF A MINOR CHORD OR THE MAJOR 3RD NOTE OF A MAJOR CHORD IS REPLACED BY THE MAJOR 2ND NOTE OR IS REPLACE BY THE PERFECT 4TH NOTE. THOUGH THERE NO RULES REGARDING HOW TO USE SUS2 AND SUS4 CHORDS (USE THE SOUNDS THAT YOU LIKE TO HEAR), GENERALLY SUS2 CHORDS ARE USED WITH ROOT (I) CHORDS AND SUS4 CHORDS ARE USED WITH FIVE (V) CHORDS. TWO OTHER SUSPENDED CHORDS EXIST: THE 7SUS2 - 1, 2, 5, b7 (NOTES) AND THE 7SUS4 - 1, 4, 5, b7 (NOTES). THESE LAST TWO (2) CHORDS ARE MORE DIFFICULT TO FRET.

GUITAR STRING LETTER NAME / STRAIGHT GUITAR TUNING (NO LOOSENING OF STRINGS / NO DROP TUNING): FROM THICKEST STRING TO THINNEST STRING: (THICKEST) E, A, D, G, B, E (THINNEST)

GRIDS WILL HELP LOCATE ROOT NOTES FOR MAJOR, MINOR, AUGMENTED, DIMINISHED 7 AND SUSPENDED 2/4 CHORDS USING ROOT NOTE LOCATION ON D, G, B, E (THINNEST) STRINGS:

ROOT		D	G	B	E	(STRING)
C	-	10	5	13	8	(FRET)
F	-	3	10	6	13	(FRET)
G	-	5	12	8	15(3)	(FRET)

ROOT		D	G	B	E	(STRING)
A	-	7	2(14)	10	5	(FRET)
D	-	12	7	3(15)	10	(FRET)
E	-	(2)14	9	5(17)	12	(FRET)

B DIMINISHED IS THE 7TH DIATONIC CHORD OF THE C MAJOR / A MINOR DIATONIC SCALE. B DIMINISHED NOTES ARE: B, D, F OR 1, b3, b5 (NOTES). HOWEVER, FOR THE USE OF SYMMETRY, BORROWED FROM THE CHROMATIC SCALE WILL BE THE bb 7TH (MAJ 6TH) NOTE: A^b ($G^\#$). B DIMINISHED 7 NOTES ARE B, D, F AND A^b OR: 1, b3, b5, bb7. AGAIN, THE IDEA OF SYMMETRY ALLOWS THE B DIMINISHED 7 CHORD TO BE MOVED THREE (3) FRETS ALONG THE GUITAR NECK AND GIVE THE SAME CHORD, WITH THE EXACT SAME SHAPE AND WITH THE EXACT SAME NOTES (NOTES ARE REARRANGED).

ROOT NOTE LOCATION ON D, G, B, E (THINNEST) STRINGS:

ROOT		D	G	B	E	(STRINGS)
B	-	9	4	12	7	(FRET)

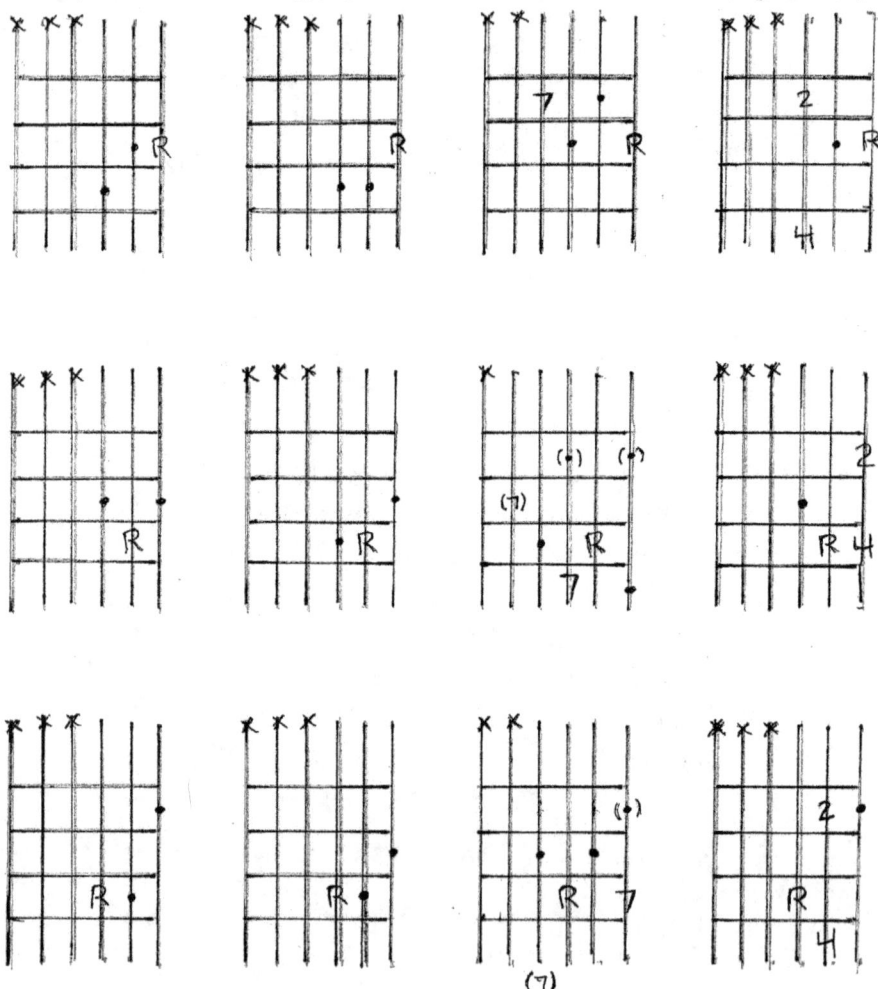

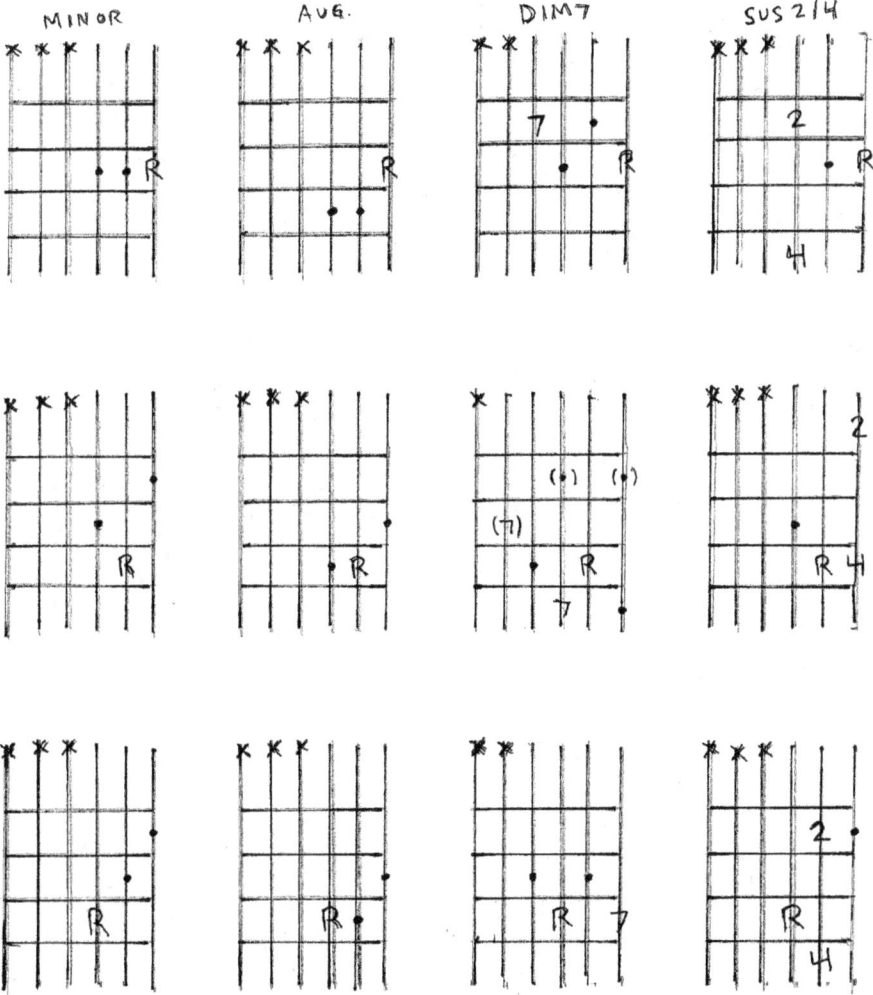

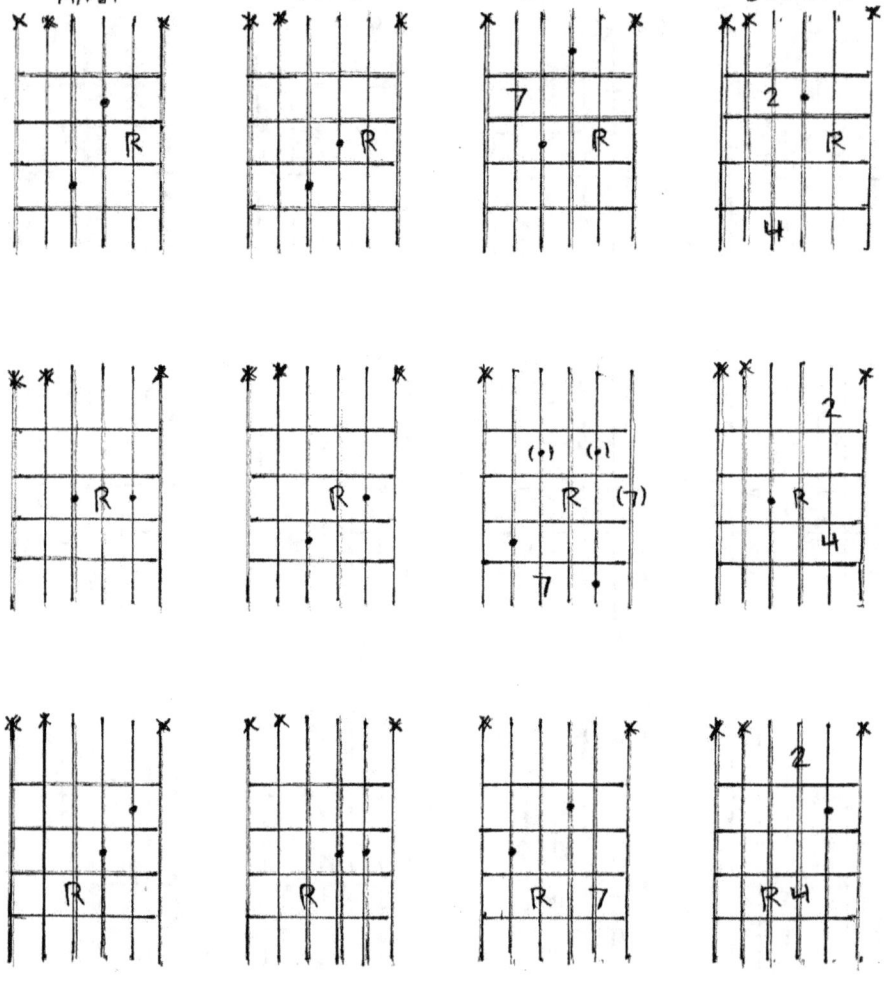

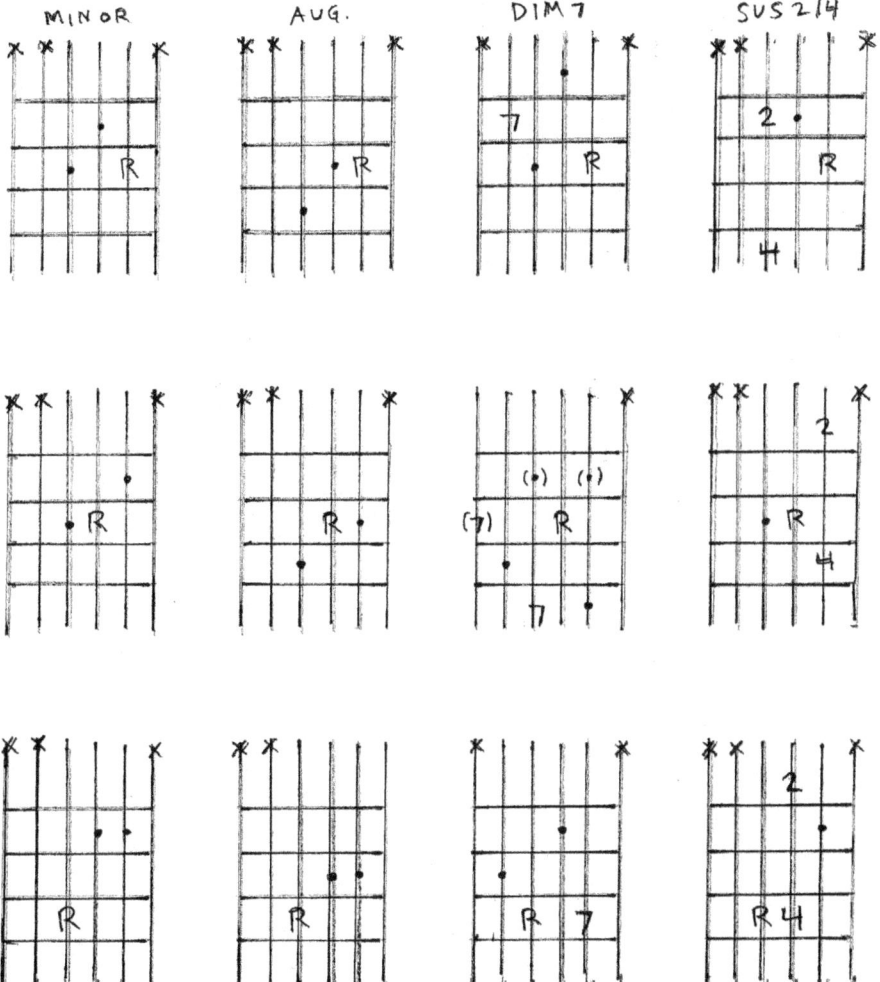

DYADS (TWO NOTE) CHORDS

DYADS, ALSO KNOWN AS DOUBLE STOPS, ARE TWO NOTES OR TWO PITCHES (Hz) PAIRED TOGETHER CREATING A SIMPLE, CONVINCING SOUND. THE MOST COMMON DOUBLE STOPS ARE 3RDS FOR ROCK N ROLL, 4THS AND 5THS FOR HARD ROCK (METAL) AND 6THS FOR COUNTRY WESTERN.

USING THE C MAJOR / A MINOR DIATONIC SCALE: C, D, E, F, G, A, B — C IS THE ONE (I) NOTE (TONIC). FOR THIRDS, START WITH THE C NOTE, COUNT TO IT'S THIRD, THE E NOTE. FOR FOURTHS, START WITH THE C NOTE, COUNT TO IT'S FOURTH, THE F NOTE. FOR FIFTHS, START WITH THE C NOTE, COUNT TO IT'S FIFTH, THE G NOTE. FOR SIXTHS, START WITH THE C NOTE, COUNT TO IT'S SIXTH, THE A NOTE. SEE THE PATTERN? START WITH ANY NOTE IN THE DIATONIC SCALE AND COUNT INTERVALS TO FORM DOUBLE STOP (DYAD) CHORDS: C, D, E, F, G, A, B : C IS I (ONE)

NOTE THE PATTERNS FORMED STARTING WITH THE C NOTE, HOW IT RELATES TO IT'S PAIRED 3RD, 4TH, 5TH, OR 6TH NOTES, THEN HOW THE RELATIONSHIP CONTINUES WITH THE REST OF THE SCALE NOTES AND THEIR PAIRED 3RD, 4TH, 5TH OR 6TH NOTES.

3RDS
C - E
D - F
E - G
F - A
G - B
A - C
B - D

5THS
C - G
D - A
E - B
F - C
G - D
A - E
B - F

4THS
C - F
D - G
E - A
F - B
G - C
A - D
B - E

6THS
C - A
D - B
E - C
F - D
G - E
A - F
B - G

3RDS

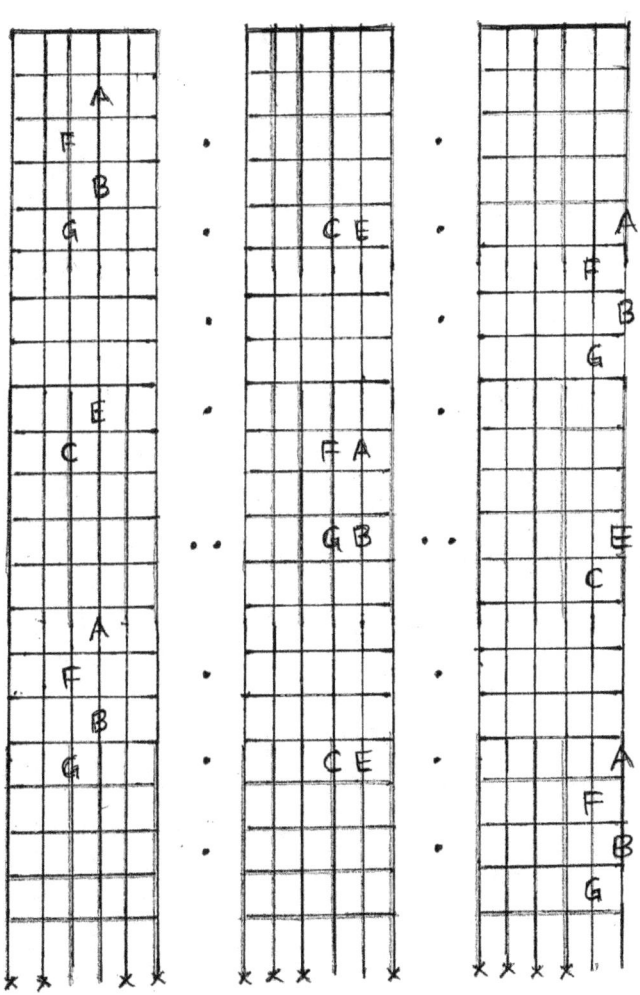

I - C, E
IV - F, A
V - G, B

3RDS

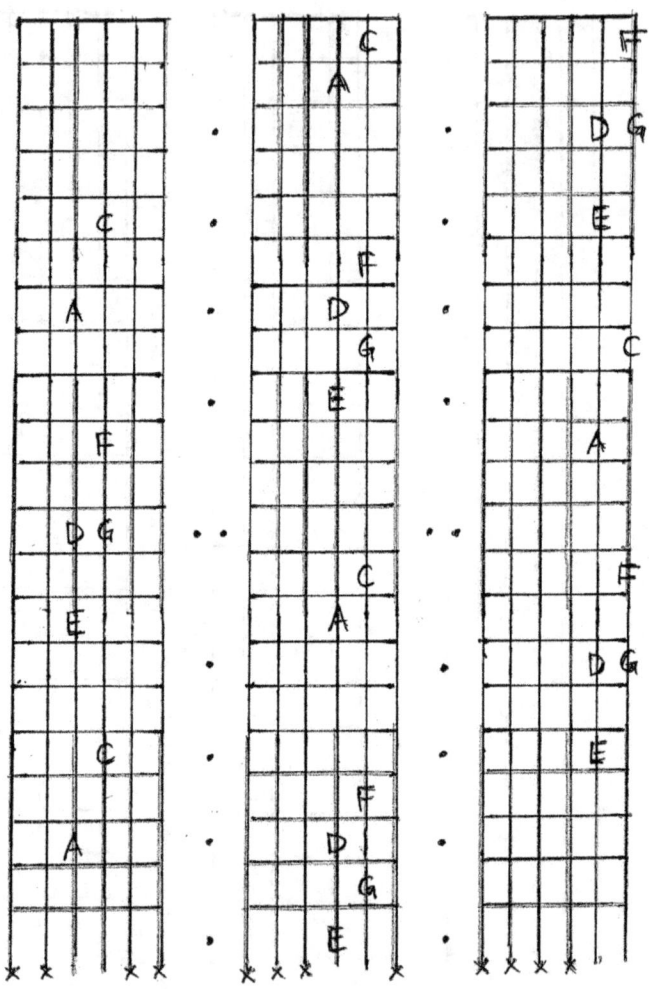

ii – D, F
iii – E, G
vi – A, C

4THS

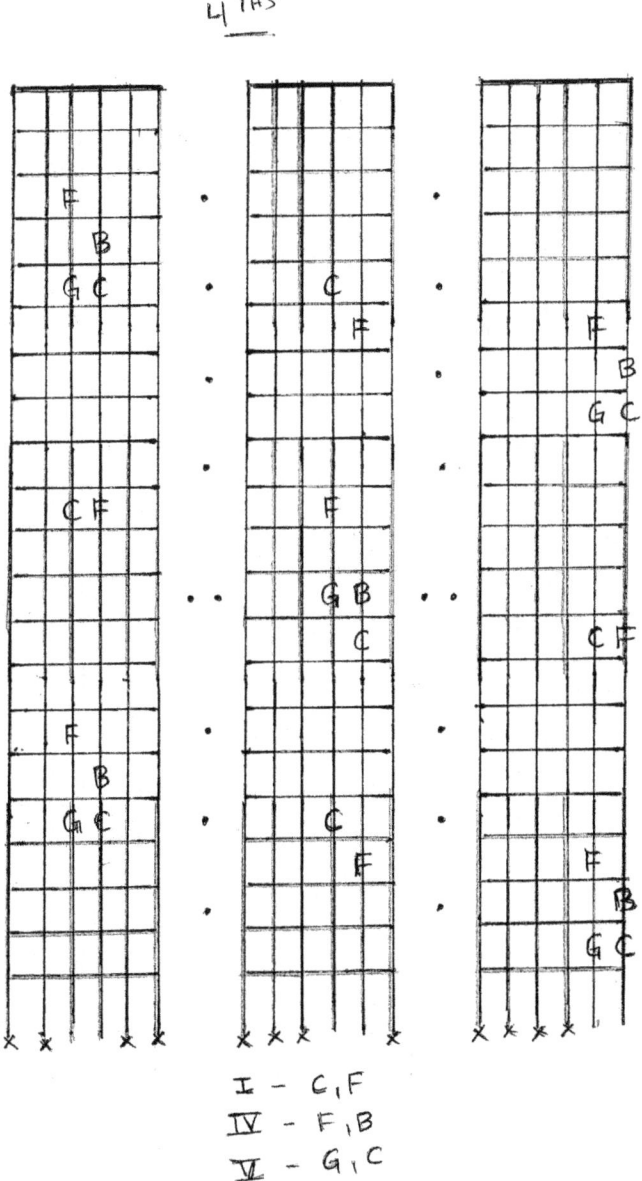

I — C, F
IV — F, B
V — G, C

4THS

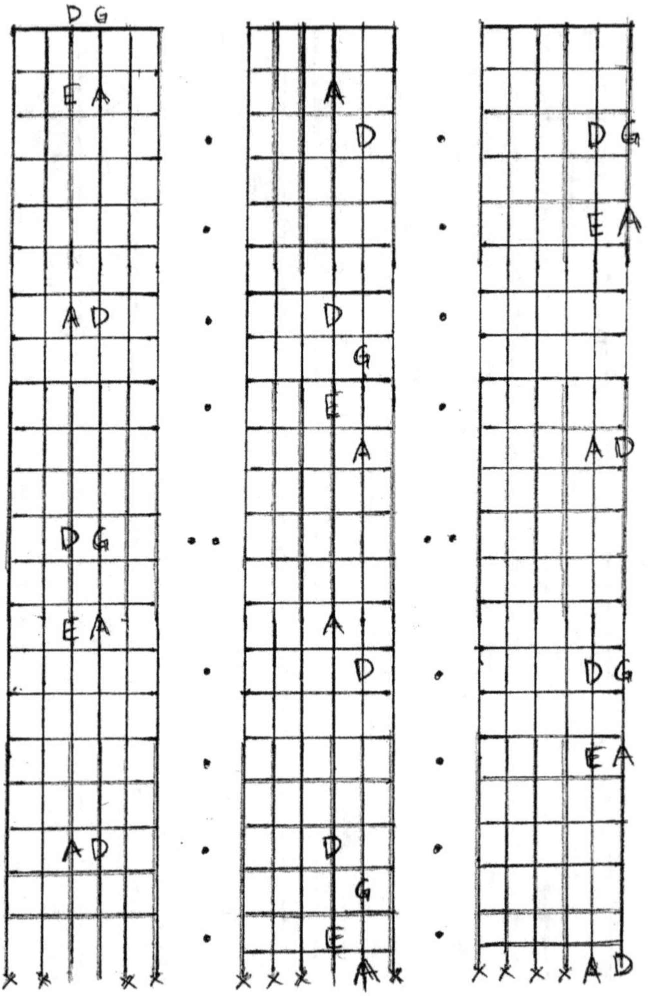

ii – D, G
iii – E, A
vi – A, D

5THS

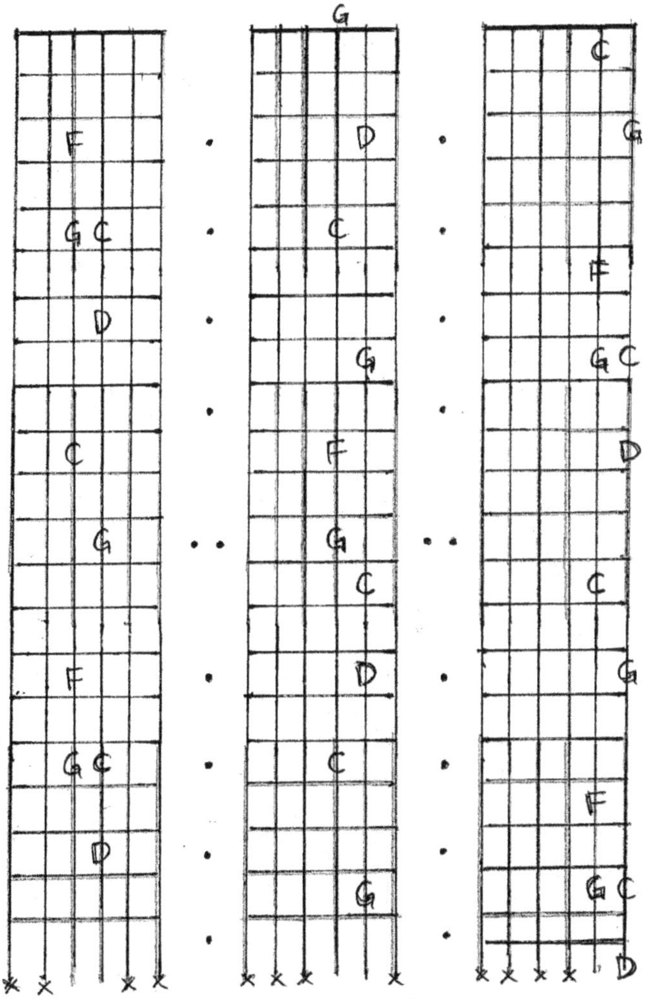

I - C, G
IV - F, C
V - G, D

5THS

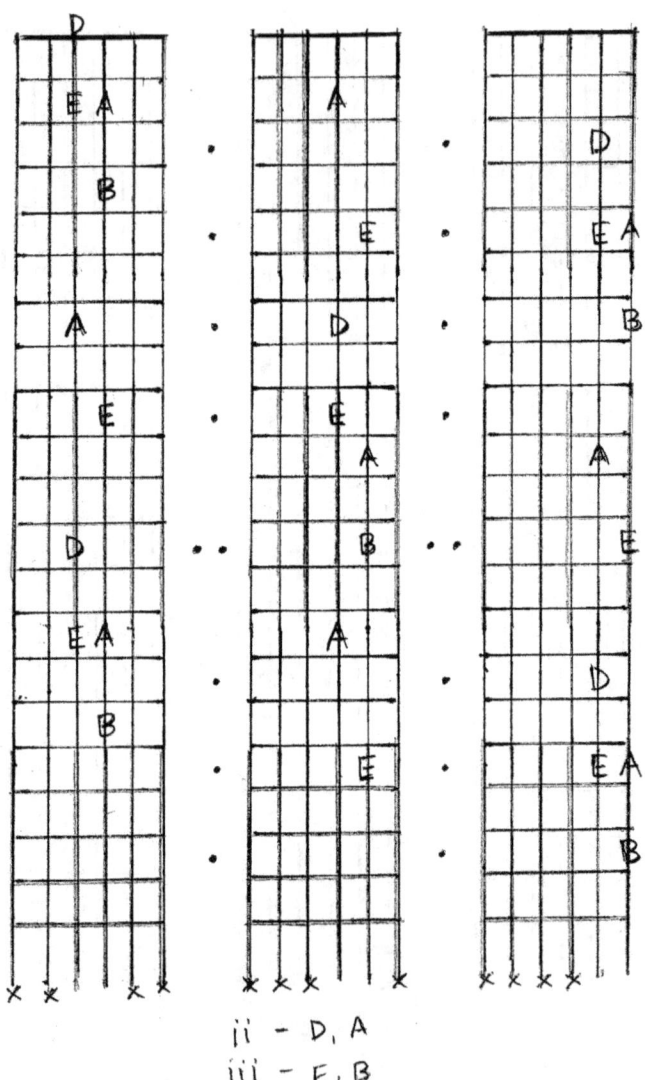

ii - D, A
iii - E, B
vi - A, E

6THS

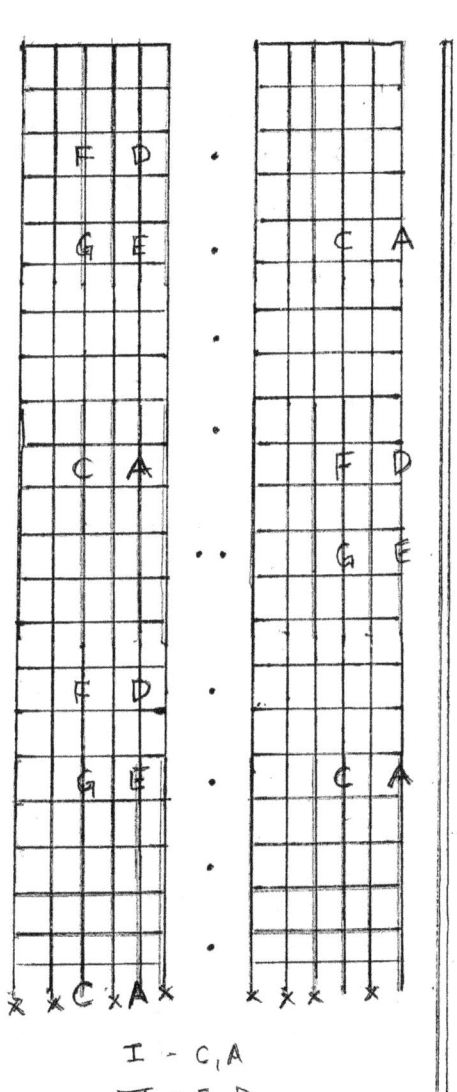
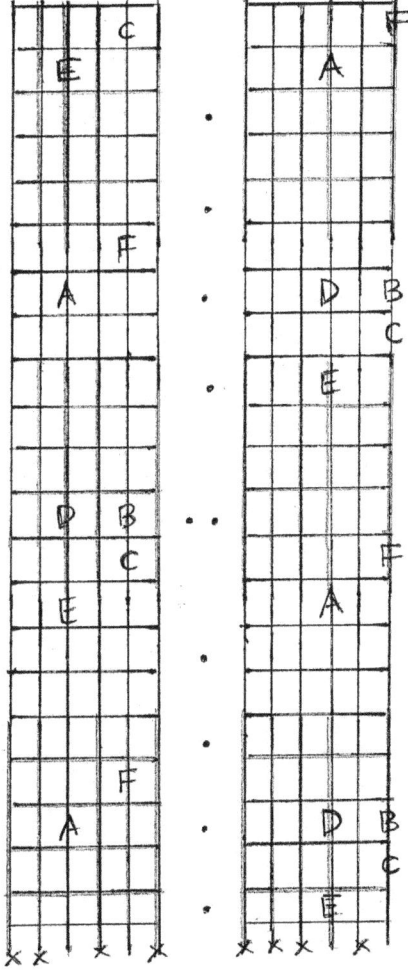

I - C,A
IV - F,D
V - G,E

ii - D,B
iii - E,C
vi - A,F

12 BAR (BLUES) RHYTHM

I	I	I	I
$IV^{7(9)}$	$IV^{7(9)}$	I	I
$V^{7(9)}$	$V^{7(9)}$	I	I

$$C - F^{7(9)} - G^{7(9)}$$
$$I - IV^{7(9)} - V^{7(9)}$$
$$A - D^{7(9)} - E^{7(9)}$$

BLUES:

MAJ

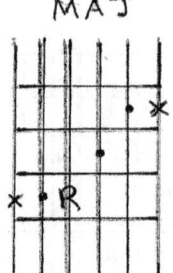

7TH

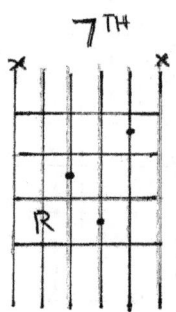

9TH

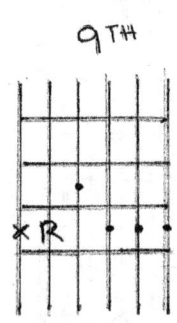

UP TO THIS POINT, C MAJOR HAS BEEN THE CHORD STUDIED, A LOT. HOWEVER, A MAJOR IS A KEY PLAYED A LOT IN BLUES SO IT MUST BE INCLUDED. IN A MAJOR, THOUGH NOTES CHANGE, THE SCALE STEPS (INTERVALS) REMAIN THE SAME AS C MAJOR. HERE WITH 12 BARS (MEASURES): THE FIRST (4) FOUR MEASURES ARE ONE (I) CHORD, THE 5TH AND 6TH MEASURES ARE FOUR ($IV^{7(9)}$) CHORD, THE 7TH AND 8TH MEASURES ARE THE ONE (I) CHORD, THE 9TH AND 10TH MEASURES ARE THE FIVE $V^{7(9)}$ CHORD AND THE 11TH AND 12TH MEASURES ARE THE ONE (I) CHORD. THIS EXAMPLE IS JUST ONE WAY OF DOZENS (MORE LIKE HUNDREDS) OF WAYS TO PLAY THE 12 BAR BLUES.

AS FOR THE ACTUAL STRUM PATTERNS USED FOR PLAYING BLUES RHYTHM, AGAIN THEY ARE DOZENS (MORE LIKE HUNDREDS) OF WAYS TO STRUM THE 12 BAR BLUES. THE BEST WAY WILL BE THE WAY YOU LIKE, THE ONE YOU CHOOSE.

NOTE: SUBSTITUTE OR MIX IN THE SEVENTH (7) CHORD WITH THE NINTH (9) CHORD.

FRET / CHORD
10 – C MAJ - R
8 < $\begin{smallmatrix}F7\\F9\end{smallmatrix}$ > R

FRET / CHORD
10 < $\begin{smallmatrix}G7\\G9\end{smallmatrix}$ > R

FRET / CHORD
7 – A MAJ - R
5 < $\begin{smallmatrix}D7\\D9\end{smallmatrix}$ > R

FRET / CHORD
7 < $\begin{smallmatrix}E7\\E9\end{smallmatrix}$ > R

DYAD 12 BAR BLUES RHYTHM (GRIDS TO FOLLOW)

STARTING IN THE KEY OF C MAJOR, THERE WILL BE THREE (3) CHORD MOVEMENTS USING ONE (1) MUSICAL RIFF; THREE (3) DOWN STRUMS AND ONE (1) HAMMER-ON (PHYSICALLY USING A FINGER TO POUND DOWN ONE (1) FRET FROM AN ALREADY RINGING NOTE, CREATING A NEW RINGING NOTE). 12 BAR (MEASURES) BLUES!

I CHORD — 1ST STRUM IS 1ST DYAD GRID: R IS C NOTE @ 8TH FRET
— 2ND STRUM IS 2ND DYAD GRID: TWO (2) FRETS FROM R @ 10TH FRET
— 3RD STRUM IS 3RD DYAD GRID: SAME FRET AS R @ 8TH FRET
— HAMMER-ON IS 3RD DYAD GRID: ONE (1) FRET FROM R @ 9TH FRET
(PLAY THIS FOUR (4) TIMES)

IV CHORD — 1ST STRUM IS 1ST DYAD GRID: R IS F NOTE @ 1ST FRET
— 2ND STRUM IS 2ND DYAD GRID: TWO (2) FRETS FROM R @ 3RD FRET
— 3RD STRUM IS 3RD DYAD GRID: SAME FRET AS R @ 1ST FRET
— HAMMER-ON IS 3RD DYAD GRID: ONE (1) FRET FROM R @ 2ND FRET
(PLAY THIS TWO (2) TIMES)

I CHORD — SAME MOVEMENT AS FIRST FOUR (4) MEASURES
(PLAY THIS TWO (2) TIMES)

V CHORD — 1ST STRUM IS 1ST DYAD GRID: R IS G NOTE @ 3RD FRET
— 2ND STRUM IS 2ND DYAD GRID: TWO (2) FRETS FROM R @ 5TH FRET
— 3RD STRUM IS 3RD DYAD GRID: SAME FRET AS R @ 3RD FRET
— HAMMER-ON IS 3RD DYAD GRID: ONE (1) FRET FROM R @ 4TH FRET
(PLAY THIS TWO (2) TIMES)

I CHORD — SAME MOVEMENT AS FIRST FOUR (4) MEASURES
(PLAY THIS TWO (2) TIMES)

DYAD 12 BAR BLUES RHYTHM SUBSTITUTIONS

I - R THE C NOTE @ 8TH FRET BECOMES 5 THE G NOTE @ 12TH FRET

IV - R THE F NOTE @ 1ST FRET BECOMES 5 THE C NOTE @ 5TH FRET

V - R THE G NOTE @ 3RD FRET BECOMES 5 THE D NOTE @ 7TH FRET

THE KEY OF C MAJOR CAN BE CHANGED TO THE KEY OF A MAJOR:

I - R THE C NOTE @ 8TH FRET BECOMES R THE A NOTE @ 5TH FRET

IV - R THE F NOTE @ 1ST FRET BECOMES R THE D NOTE @ 10TH FRET

V - R THE G NOTE @ 3RD FRET BECOMES R THE E NOTE @ 12TH FRET

STAYING IN KEY OF A MAJOR (SUBSTITUTIONS):

I - R THE A NOTE @ 5TH FRET BECOMES 5 THE E NOTE @ 9TH FRET

IV - R THE D NOTE @ 10TH FRET BECOMES 5 THE A NOTE @ 14TH FRET

V - R THE E NOTE @ 12TH FRET BECOMES 5 THE B NOTE @ 16TH FRET

HERE'S WHAT IS BEING PLAYED: 1ST DYAD GRID - ROOT NOTE AND PERFECT 5TH, 2ND DYAD GRID - MAJOR 6TH AND PERFECT 4TH, 3RD DYAD GRID - PERFECT 5TH AND MINOR 3RD, HAMMER-ON IS MAJOR 3RD. SUBSTITUTION IS: PERFECT 5TH AND MINOR 7TH.

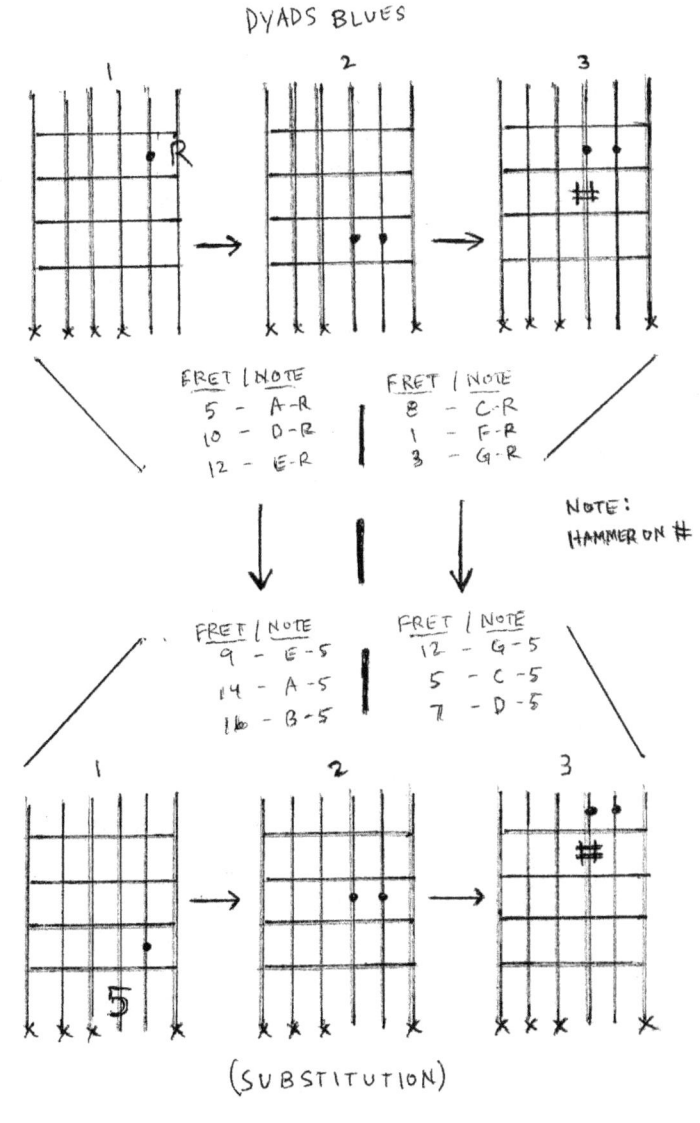

DYADS / DOUBLE STOPS FOR BLUES

The grids that follow will be in C Major / A minor using the chromatic scale. The chromatic scale will allow the two-note chords to give a real blues sound. With all that's been studied, the introduction of these rootless (lack of the one (I) note) chords should be an easy breakdown and understanding. The chromatic interval chart studied thus far will help make sense of these chords. The double stop blues grids contain 6th, 7th and 9th chords. These chords are useful to have, to add variance to your guitar rhythms and your lead solos. They add punch to any measure of music!

The idea of using these chords, or any notes for that matter, to create melodies within chord progressions is a treasure waiting to be found! Start simple and the more you practice, the better (at playing) you'll get, and the more complex you'll get.

Again, these grids are in C Major / A minor. However, these chords can be transposed to any musical key desired (either change root note and start anew or simply count fret distance between old and new root notes and apply the same fret distance between any desired note in scale or chord.

In addition, notes and chords, especially two-note chords will sometimes overlap into other keys and be used as different notes at different intervals (scale steps). That's normal! What counts is that the notes or chords within the key you're playing are technically sound, and most important, sound good to you!

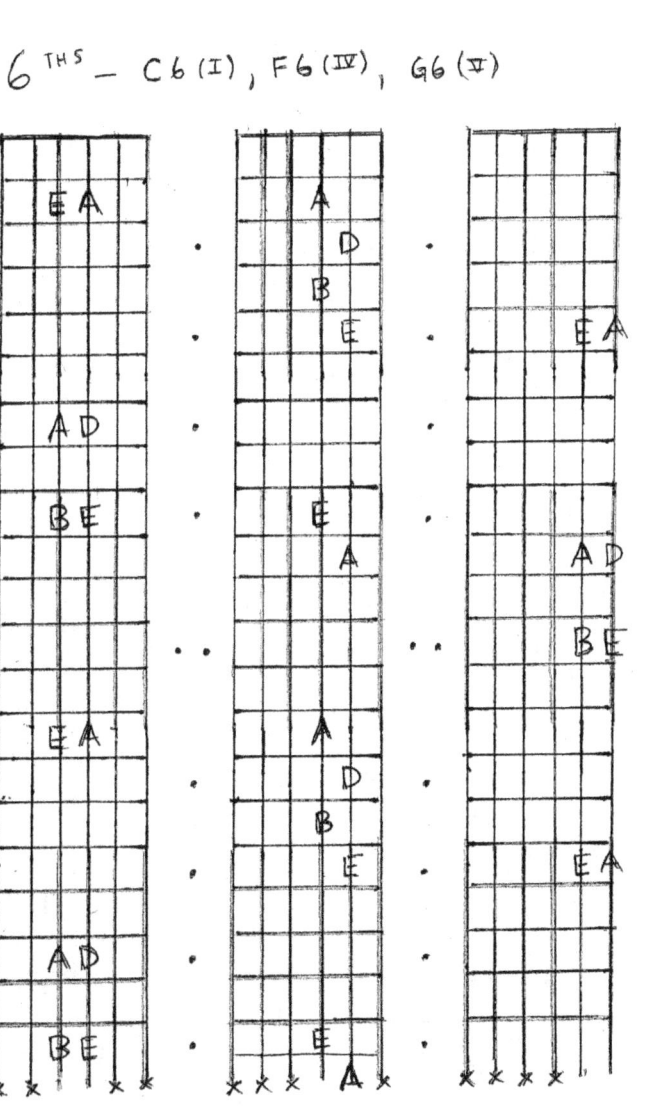

6^{THS} — Dm6 (ii), Em6 (iii), Am6 (vi)

ii — F, B
MINOR 3RD, MAJ 6TH
(Dm6)

iii — G, C#
MINOR 3RD, MAJ 6TH
(Em6)

vi — C, F#
MINOR 3RD, MAJ 6TH
(Am6)

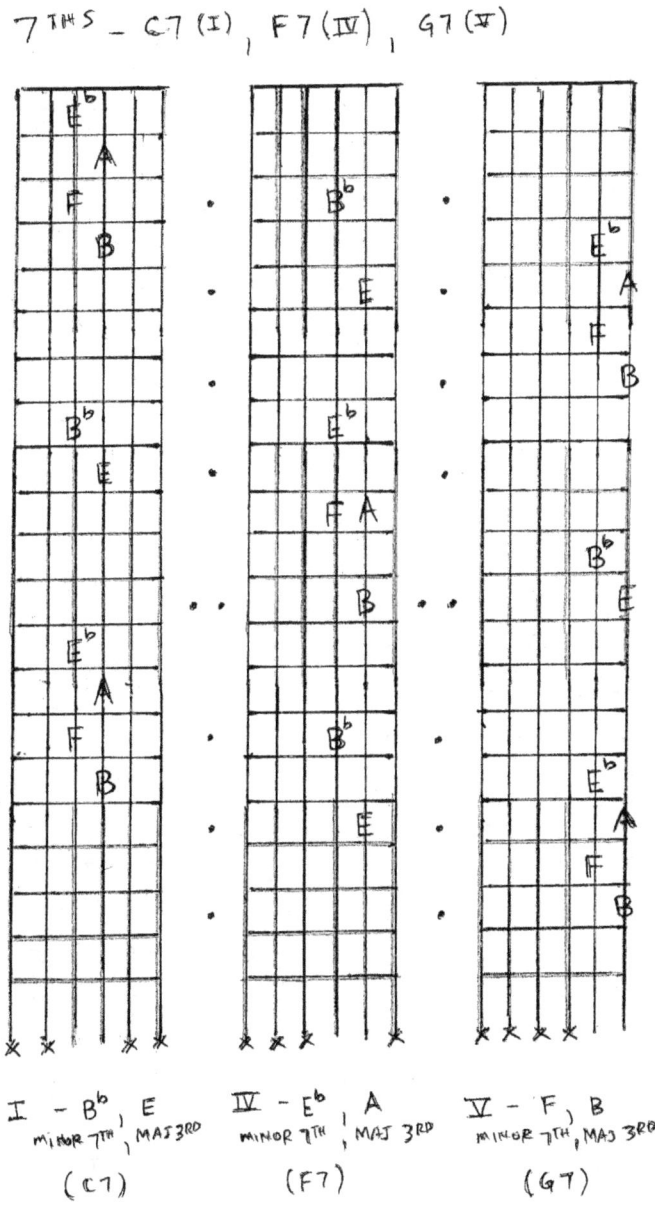

7THS — Dm7(ii), Em7(iii), Am7(vi)

ii — C, F
MINOR 7TH, MINOR 3RD
(Dm7)

iii — D, G
MINOR 7TH, MINOR 3RD
(Em7)

vi — G, C
MINOR 7TH, MINOR 3RD
(Am7)

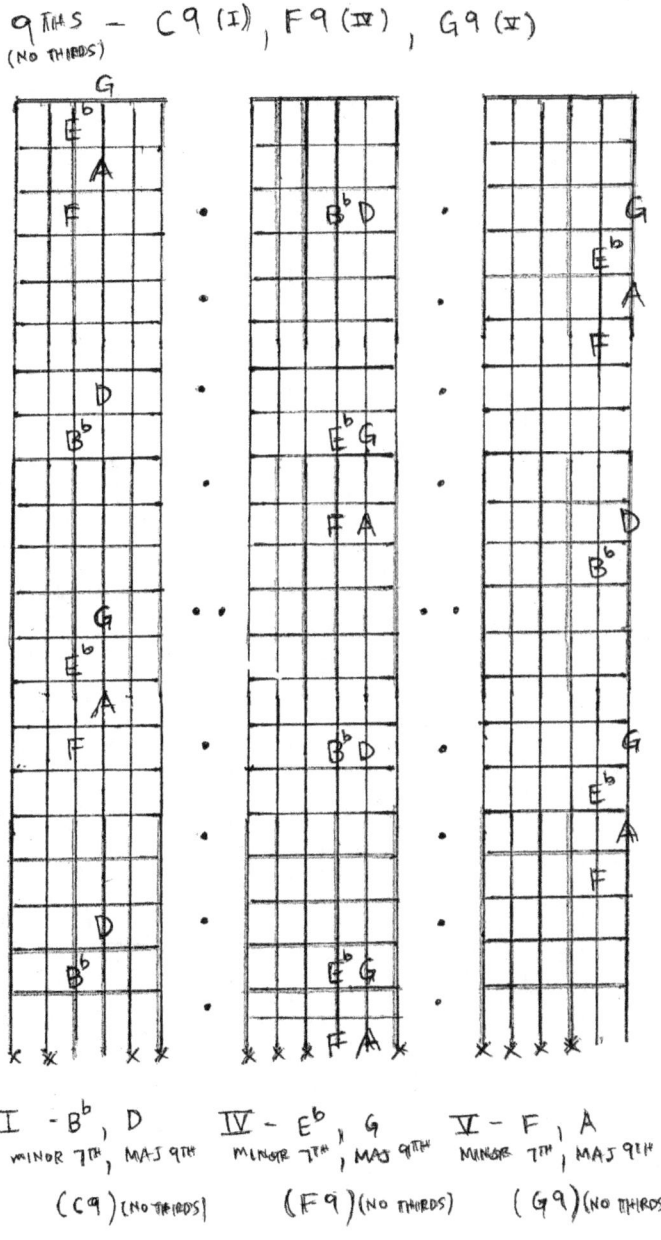

9THS — Dm9(ii), Em9(iii), Am9(vi)
(NO THIRDS)

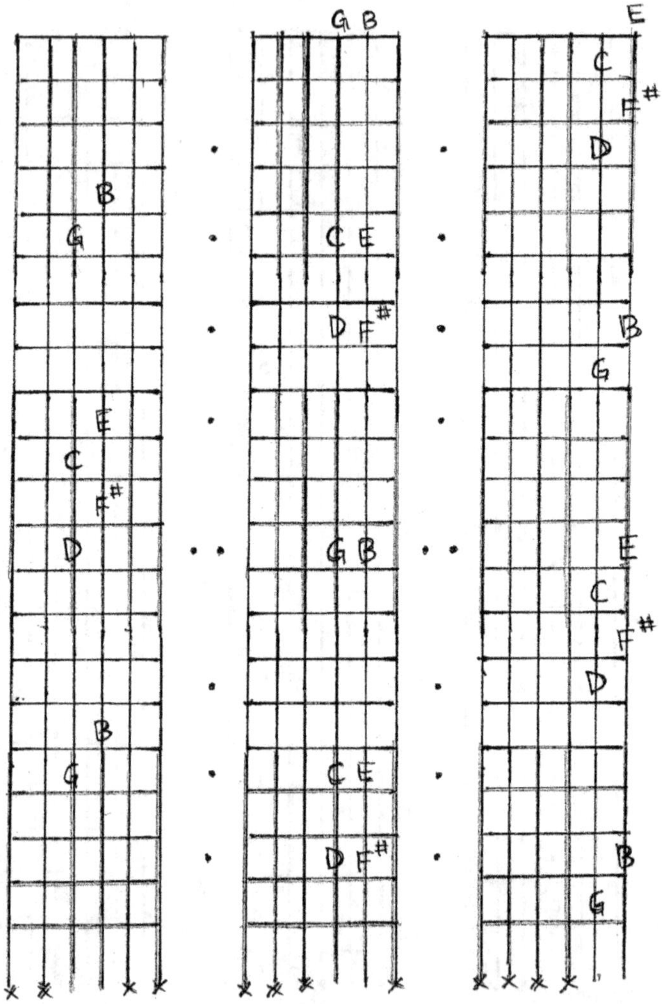

ii – C, E
MINOR 7TH, MAJ 9TH
(Dm9) (NO THIRDS)

iii – D, F#
MINOR 7TH, MAJ 9TH
(Em9) (NO THIRDS)

vi – G, B
MINOR 7TH, MAJ 9TH
(Am9) (NO THIRDS)

7 SEVEN NOTE CHORD KEYS

KEY	I	ii	iii	IV	V	vi	vii dim
C -	C	Dm	Em	F	G	Am	B°
D -	D	Em	F#m	G	A	Bm	C#°
E -	E	F#m	G#m	A	B	C#m	D#°
F -	F	Gm	Am	B♭	C	Dm	E°
G -	G	Am	Bm	C	D	Em	F#°
A -	A	Bm	C#m	D	E	F#m	G#°
B -	B	C#m	D#m	E	F#	G#m	A#°

NOTE - MAJOR CHORD KEYS ARE LISTED WITH THEIR DIATONIC CHORDS. NOTICE HOW THE SEVEN (7) ROOT LETTER NAMES OF EACH CHORD IN A KEY BECOMES THE SAME SEVEN (7) LETTER NAMES FOR EACH NOTE OF THE KEY'S MAJOR SCALE!

C MAJOR SCALE: C, D, E, F, G, A, B

(7) SEVEN NOTE GUITAR RELATES A SMALL SET OF SCALE NOTES TO THE SIMPLEST OF CHORDS. THIS RELATIONSHIP ALLOWS THE READER TO MAKE SENSE OF HOW ALL CHORDS RELATE TO SCALES, HOW CHORDS RELATE TO RELATIVE CHORDS FOUND WITHIN THE SAME SCALE, AND HOW WHEN REARRANGED, THE SAME SCALE NOTES (CALLED MODES) ALLOW FOR THE RE-ARRANGEMENT OF CHORD SEQUENCES (CALLED PROGESSIONS).

IN ADDITION, WHILE STUDYING WITHIN ONE SIMPLE SCALE, (7) SEVEN NOTE GUITAR CONTAINS NUMEROUS MOVABLE GRIDS, INCLUDING A VARIETY OF TWO NOTE DYAD CHORDS DESCRIBED IN DETAIL, COMPLETE COMMON THREE NOTE TRIAD CHORDS, AS WELL AS BARRE CHORDS AND OPEN CHORDS. USING BASIC SIMPLE CHORDS ALLOWS FOR RELATING THEIR PRECISE ABILITIES AS COMBINED NOTES TO BETTER UNDERSTAND THEIR RELATIONSHIP WITHIN A SCALE; THUS, ALLOWING THE READER TO MAKE BETTER SENSE OF HOW MUSIC IS MADE. FURTHERMORE, THE IDEA OF UNDERSTANDING MUSIC AND ITS SIMPLE STRUCTURE ALLOWS LEARNING MORE COMPLEX MUSIC, WHETHER IT'S YOUR FAVORITE ARTIST'S MUSIC OR MAKING YOUR OWN MUSIC, TO BE A VERY ENJOYABLE EXPERIENCE.